T0228063

THE INDIE GAME DEVELOPER HANDBOOK

THE INDIE GAME DEVELOPER HANDBOOK

Richard Hill-Whittall

Routledge
Taylor & Francis Group

LONDON AND NEW YORK

First published 2015 by Focal Press

2 Park Square, Milton Park, Abingdon, Oxon OX14 4RN
711 Third Avenue, New York, NY 10017, USA

Routledge is an imprint of the Taylor & Francis Group, an informa business

First issued in hardback 2017

Library of Congress Cataloging-in-Publication Data

Hill-Whittall, Richard.
   The indie game developer handbook / Richard Hill-Whittall.
      pages cm
   Includes bibliographical references.
   1. Computer games—Programming.   I. Title.
   QA76.76.C672H55 2015
   794.8'1526—dc23
   2014033755

ISBN: 978-1-138-82842-1 (pbk)
ISBN: 978-1-138-42819-5 (hbk)

Typeset in Minion Pro
By Apex CoVantage, LLC

Contents

Indie Game
Development

The Best Job in the World!

Indie game development is a wonderful, exciting and incredibly rewarding job. It offers a world of possibilities and promise, and with careful planning and perhaps a little luck, you can earn decent regular revenue and begin building up a successful studio.

It has never been easier to develop a game, thanks to the wide range of development SDKs such as Unity 3D, Game Maker and Unreal that are now available. The opportunities to self-publish your own games are many and varied—you can create the game you want to create and know that you can get it to market on a large array of different devices, including PCs, consoles and mobiles.

Be prepared to persevere; often your first game will only bring you limited returns, yet your first published title acts as a vital initial step in building up a catalogue of titles, expanding your community of followers and ultimately earning a solid regular income.

I started out developing video games in 1995, at a company called Silltunna Software. My first game was called XTreme Racing for the Commodore Amiga, and my primary role was artist and track designer. I also dipped my toe in the water in other areas, such as PR, business development and marketing. I knew from that point on that this was what I wanted to do more than anything else in the world.

Since I was about 10 years old, video games have been my passion. I would spend hours playing games on my first computer, a ZX Spectrum, dreaming about one day creating my own games. Here I am, nearly 30 years later, doing just that—and I have been for the last 18-ish years.

During that time, I have managed the development of, and released, 33 games over 44 different SKUs. In addition to running the development of those games, I was also the lead artist, game designer and sound designer. It has been an incredible, wonderful and terrifying experience, and I consider myself incredibly lucky to be able to do what I do for a job.

I have self-published 14 of those games, which looking back now seems unbelievable. True, some titles make little money, but the personal reward and enjoyment from creating each game, getting that final product out there is just incredible.

What greater incentive can there be than to know that if you keep creating games, keep doing the job you love, that one day you may earn enough money to change your life forever? Sure, it's a longshot—but that glimmer is always there.

I have made a whole bunch of mistakes and learned a lot of lessons the hard way. I have released some games I am really pleased with, and others that I am not. Through it all I have always loved the day-to-day development process; creating new games, learning new techniques, sourcing new content. To me this is the best job in the world!

What I have tried to do with this book is to document every single aspect of indie game development. I have included expert advice from other studios and industry professionals, along with my own personal experiences of running an indie game development studio over the last 18 years. My hope is that this book will provide a useful knowledge base and help to support the learning process of running an indie development studio, allowing you to focus on creating amazing, fun and well-received games.

I'd like to say a big thank you to the following sites and individuals, all of whom provide amazing insight and resources for indie developers:

Pixel Prospector (http://www.pixelprospector.com)
What can I say? THE best site on the internet if you are an indie game developer.

Gamasutra (http://www.gamasutra.com)
An incredibly useful treasure trove of information, advice and firsthand development experiences.

Game Academy (https://www.gameacademy.com)
Excellent selection of game development, PR and marketing help and advice articles.

Cliff Harris/Positech (http://positech.co.uk/cliffsblog)
A no-nonsense guy with a lot of great advice for indies.

Develop (http://www.develop-online.net)
Another great resource for indie development info.

Tigsource (http://forums.tigsource.com)
A fantastic discussion forum with a very active and helpful indie community.

Harry van Horen at Rangeela (http://www.rangeela.nl)
For always being 100% reliable and a very nice guy.

Jay Koottarappallil at WhiteMoon Dreams
A big thanks to Jay for his help and insight.

Harry Holmwood
An insightful and thoroughly good guy.

Agostino Simonetta
For being the best guy in the industry, who had helped me out a lot.

Alex Chapman
A decent guy and very good game lawyer, who had helped many indie studios over the years.

Danny Flexner
Great artist with a good eye for marketing.
Fancy a chat? Drop me an email to rich@supericon.co.uk. For regular updates you can also visit the official book site at http://www. indiegamedevbook.com/
On that note, let's begin . . .

CHAPTER 1

Development Tools and Resources

Game Development Systems

When I first started creating games there was really only one choice for development, and that was to create your own engine. As such, when I began creating games, my studio developed and maintained our own cross-platform engine. Initially this engine was created for PlayStation 2 and PC development, and later expanded to cover PSP, PSVita and Wii. While having our own engine did present us with opportunities to get games published, it was also a complete and utter nightmare to maintain. Months and months were spent creating, optimizing, fixing and tweaking the engine for each new platform, and during those times we would be financially wiped out due to the time and resources it took to get the engine to support those new platforms and features.

Although we still use a version of this engine for some of our development, our focus has shifted now to using third-party tech for the future. We are currently using Unity extensively, and it is a revelation. No more waiting for features to be added to the engine, now I can just focus on creating games. I would say that my stress levels have dropped about 90% in day-to-day development. I get to focus on the cool stuff like adding new game features, nice graphical effects, fun and quirky content, social functionality—basically all of the important stuff that makes a game.

I would strongly advise against creating and maintaining your own proprietary game engine. Save grey hairs, milestone headaches and all-round frustration—grab an existing game engine and just have fun creating games!

I'm not alone in saying this either; throughout the book you will find Q&As with various other development studios, most of whom are now using third-party engines, even those that at one point used to maintain their own tech.

Let's take a look at some of the most popular solutions out there. I will cover the ones that I have used, or have had recommended to me, and for each I list the good and bad points that I am aware of. My advice would be to make sure you try out a few development solutions first, before making a final choice for your game. You may well stick with your chosen engine for many games, so make sure you make the right selection from the beginning.

I'll start with my current preference, Unity.

Unity

What They Say

"Unity is a game development ecosystem: a powerful rendering engine fully integrated with a complete set of intuitive tools and rapid workflows to create interactive 3D content; easy multiplatform publishing; thousands of quality, ready-made assets in the Asset Store and a knowledge-sharing Community.

For independent developers and studios, Unity's democratizing ecosystem smashes the time and cost barriers to creating uniquely beautiful games. They are using Unity to build a livelihood doing what they love: creating games that hook and delight players on any platform."

Platforms

Free/Pro: Windows, Mac, Linux, iOS, Android (including OUYA), Windows Phone 8, Blackberry 10, Web

Other licences are available, including PS3, PS4, PSVita, Xbox360, Xbox One—be warned though that these can be very expensive and you need to speak to Unity directly to negotiate. From what I understand, they may be flexible on how they structure the financials.

Wii-U—a Wii-U specific Unity Pro licence is supplied by Nintendo with each Wii-U development system purchased, which is a fantastic initiative by Nintendo.

Xbox One—Microsoft have confirmed that Unity will also be free for all Xbox One developers.

Unity is also free for all current Playstation systems - PS4, PS3 and PSVita.

Purchase Options
A fully featured version of Unity is available for free, and this is sufficient for just about any game type you wish to develop.

The price for a Unity Pro licence is $1500, and additional modules have to be purchased for iOS and Android. Pro versions of Windows Phone 8, Windows Store Apps and Blackberry 10 are included within the Unity Pro licence. Each of the modules also costs $1500 and you are not allowed to mix licences (i.e. you can't have a Unity Pro licence for PC but just use the free licence for iOS or Android). Also the prices are per seat—so each member of the team requires a separate licence. As you can see—the costs for going 'Pro' can swiftly get very expensive indeed.

That said though, Pro has a lot of excellent features, and if you want to make something look 'AAA' quality you will need a Pro licence to use post processing effects, advanced lighting and real-time soft shadows.

Some of the additional Pro features include:
► Custom splash screen
► LOD support
► RT soft shadows
► Post-processing effects
► Video playback
► Profiling (although there is a basic profiler available for the free version, called Benchy Profiler, available on the App Store)

I would definitely recommend Unity now above all other development platforms. Frankly, it is insane what you can do with Unity now—and all for free. Incredible! Unity Technologies have changed the industry in a profound and positive way, so bravo to them.

Developer

Unity Technologies
http://unity3D.com/

Example Games

A few examples of well-known indie Unity games (there are a LOT of Unity titles out there!):

- Call of Duty®: Strike Team
- Rain
- Kerbal Space Program
- Dead Trigger
- Deus Ex: The Fall
- Fightback
- Blitzkrieg 3
- Scrolls
- Year Walk
- Space Hulk
- The Room
- Bad Piggies
- Wasteland 2

Pros

- Free licence covers most platforms, and is fully functional.
- Unity Asset Store is an incredible resource for code, art, audio and more.
- Full 2D and 3D support, everything from simplistic styling through to AAA quality is achievable.
- There is a huge community of Unity users; as such, there is a wealth of good quality tutorials out there to help learn Unity.

Cons

- Pro licences are not cheap.
- PlayStation licences are insanely expensive.
- You need to be able to program to really take full advantage of Unity.
- Unity can be a resource hog, sometimes causing your development machine to grind to a halt. I speak from experience!

Unity Asset Store

One of the best aspects of Unity is the Asset Store—this is an incredible resource of 3D artwork, animation, particles, textures, sound, scripts, editor extensions and even full game kits you can use and adapt.

You can save many months of work often for just a few dollars by purchasing assets off the store. Many of the assets are of an incredibly high standard; I really can't recommend it highly enough. A few highlights from the store include:

- 2D Toolkit
- 2D Platform Controller
- Core GameKit
- Playmaker
- Rotorz Tile System
- Score Flash
- TextFX
- Ultimate FPS Camera
- Vectrosity
- WarFX

Insider Indie Q&A

1. *What is the name of your studio?*

   Demigiant

   DEMIGIANT
   © Daniele Giardini

2. *What year was your studio founded and what are the names of the founders?*

   2014. Founded by me (Daniele Giardini) right after I closed my previous studio (Holoville, which existed since 2004).

3. *What are the studio's key game titles?*

   Goscurry, Stackout, Journeyballs

4. *Do you have your own in-house engine or use a third party system? If third party, which one do you use?*

   I use Unity (and in the past Flash for smaller games). Both because I like its workflow and because it makes it easier to develop for multiple platforms.

5. *Which platforms do you release on now / plan to release on?*

   As of now I released on browser/PC/Linux/Mac, and will soon release for Android/iOS.

6. *Which is your most successful platform so far?*

   Browser: I released free versions of my games there, so it's an easy win.

7. *What are the development tools you use most (i.e. 2D, 3D software, audio tools etc.)?*

   Visually, Pyxel Edit for pixelart, Xara Designer Pro for vector art, Blender for 3D, Photoshop for digital painting and the rest.

   Coding-wise, I usually use Visual Studio for assemblies and Sublime Text for the rest.

   Audio-wise, I rely on Isak J Martinsson or Luigi di Guida for music and sound effects, and I have no idea what they're using, but it's cool.

   And then Unity, obviously.

8. *What advice would you give to a new studio?*

   Start by planning your first game, your marketing strategy and your future. Then keep to your schedule and aim to release as soon as possible. Most of all, though, try to find your own personal voice.

9. *What marketing resources do you use?*

   As of now I use mostly word-of-mouth and IndieDB, which surprisingly worked greatly in granting me reviews from important game magazines, but not so well for sales (even if we're only talking of Alpha pre-sales).

10. *What is your favourite indie games site?*

    Indiegames.com

11. *Are there any mistakes/hiccups you have made so far, something you would advise a new studio to avoid?*

    Don't stray too far from your initial concept (as long as the prototype was actually good): you will probably just waste your time and possibly ruin the cohesion of the game. Also, knowing your limits is very important: expand them day by day, but always keep them in mind.

GameMaker Studio

What They Say

"GameMaker: Studio caters to entry-level novices and seasoned game development professionals equally, allowing them to create cross-platform games in record time and at a fraction of the cost!

In addition to making games development 80% faster than coding for native languages, developers can create fully functional prototypes in just a few hours, and a full game in just a matter of weeks."

Platforms

Windows, Mac, Linux, iOS, Android, Windows Phone 8, HTML5, PlayStation 3, 4 and Vita

Purchase Options

Windows and Mac—two options available (Standard and Professional), with Standard now available free of charge.

Linux, iOS, Android, Windows Phone 8 and HTML 5 require the Master Collection, which is currently priced at $799.99, or you can buy export modules separately.

Developer

YoYo Games
http://yoyogames.com/

Example Games

A few examples of well-known indie GameMaker games:

- ▶ Spelunky
- ▶ Hydorah
- ▶ Super Crate Box
- ▶ Hotline Miami
- ▶ Stealth Bastard
- ▶ Gunpoint
- ▶ Home

GameMaker is a nice system for creating 2D pixel games—it is designed by game industry veterans and it shows. Features such as a solid built-in tile map editor make it one of the best 2D choices out there. The in-built scripting language is fairly easy to use, and you can author an entire game just with the drag and drop interface if the thought of coding scares you off.

Pros

▶ An excellent selection of built-in 2D tools and routines.

▶ Good and friendly support via the YoYo forums.

▶ Nice built-in scripting language that is easily to learn for beginners.

Cons

▶ The Master Collection cost is overly expensive.

Thanks to recent developments, I am getting more and more excited about GameMaker. The first bit of good news is that YoYo have finally opened an asset store, called the YoYo Marketplace. It is still early days yet, but this is such a positive step. As with the Unity Asset Store, the YoYo Marketplace is split into categories, where you can buy art, audio, extensions, scripts and full projects. I am optimistic that YoYo will continue to add more content to the Marketplace, and my feeling is that GameMaker will become a viable alternative to Unity. I would add though, that I still think YoYo need to reconsider their pricing for the Master Collection!

The other GameMaker news, and this is the biggie, is that they have added PlayStation export modules, and right now, they are free to licenced PlayStation developers. This is amazing news, and several high-profile indie titles are being developed in GameMaker now and on the way to PlayStation, including Vlambeer's Nuclear Throne, and Dennaton Games's Hotline Miami 2.

So if you would like to release on PlayStation 3, 4 or Vita, right now GameMaker is the best choice if you are on a budget.

Unreal Engine 4

What They Say

"Unreal Engine 4 is a professional suite of tools and technologies used for building high-quality games across a range of platforms. Unreal Engine 4's rendering architecture enables developers to achieve stunning visuals and also scale elegantly to lower-end systems.

Revolutionary new workflow features and a deep toolset empower developers to quickly iterate on ideas and see immediate results, while complete C++ source code access brings the experience to a whole new level."

Platforms

Unreal Engine 4 subscription enables you to deploy to Windows PC, Mac, iOS and Android. Xbox One and PS4 console support is available to subscribers who are registered developers for the respective platform.

Price

Unreal Engine is offered under a subscription plan at $19 per month. Once you ship your game, you then need to pay 5% of gross revenue to Epic Games.

Developer

Epic Games
https://www.unrealengine.com/

Example Games

► Daylight
► Rime
► Last Knight
► Gunner Z
► Tower of Ascension
► Antichamber

Pros

► Visually it is hard to top the Unreal Engine—'AAA' quality all the way.
► A wide range of systems, including consoles supported.
► Amazing built-in middleware and top-notch post-production effects.
► Good community support and lots of online tutorials available.

Cons

► Licence fee structure can make Unreal Engine expensive if your game sells well.
► Many users report a steep learning curve; Unreal Engine is certainly one of the more complex development kits out there.
► Lack of an asset store.

Construct 2

What They Say

"Construct 2 is a powerful ground breaking HTML5 game creator designed specifically for 2D games. It allows anyone to build games—no coding required!

It's great for beginners, and powerful enough to let experts work even quicker than by coding!"

Platforms
Windows, Mac, Linux, iOS*, Android*, Blackberry 10, HTML5
(*via the free CocoonJS and Direct Canvas third party solutions)

Purchase Options
There is a restricted free version that limits certain features and only allows you to publish non-commercially on Windows 8 Metro, Facebook and Chrome.

There is a Personal Edition that is just for individual use, although it does allow for commercial usage.

And finally, there is a Business Edition, which offers full/unlimited usage.

Developer
Scirra
https://www.scirra.com/construct2

Example Games
- ► Super Ubi Land
- ► 8bit Boy
- ► Drunken Wizard

Pros
- ► Construct 2 is a good, cost-effective solution for simple 2D games.
- ► It has a number of built-in classes, such as a Platform Game class, which provide core functionality such as slopes, moving platforms, "jump-thru" platforms and arbitrary angles of gravity.
- ► One of the most non-coder friendly options out there, so can be a great choice if you do not wish to touch code in any way.
- ► Ideal solution for rapid prototyping of concepts.

Cons
- ► Not really suitable for complex games.
- ► Scripting support is not the best, apparently a little buggy and lacking in features.

Insider Indie Q&A

1. *What is the name of your studio?*

   Kybele Studio

2. *What year was your studio founded and what are the names of the founders?*

   Founded in 2012 by Dhaunae De Vir and Julio Romacho.

3. *What are the studio's key game titles?*

   Cannon Ball Pest Control and Crazy Market Karts.

4. *Do you have your own in-house engine or use a third party system? If third party, which one do you use?*

   We have been mostly working with Unity 3D and Construct 2.

5. *Which platforms do you release on now / plan to release on?*

   Right now we are working on browser games for laptops, iPhone apps and OUYA.

6. *Which is your most successful platform so far?*

   Browser games are really accessible.

7. *What are the development tools you use most (i.e. 2D, 3D software, audio tools etc.)?*

   Photoshop and Illustrator are a must, as well as 3D Studio. For actual programming, just your preferred IDE.

8. *What advice would you give to a new studio?*

   Try to make a multidisciplinary team with at least a game designer, a graphic artist, a sound composer and a coder. If one person can fulfil more than one role in a small project, that's fine. It is essential to adapt the number of team members to the scope of the project in order to make the workflow smoother and faster. Always make sure everyone is truly committed to your studio.

9. *What marketing resources do you use?*

   Facebook and Twitter are the easiest (and cheapest) resources right now, and really useful in getting your games viral.

10. *What are your favourite indie games sites?*

Desura is our go-to place when I want to look at commercialised titles, as well as the Greenlight part of Steam. Additionally, bundle-type sites (Humble Bundle, Indie Gala and so on) are pretty useful to discover studios and their products. For our mini-game and browser game's needs, we always go to Kongregate.

Clickteam Fusion

What They Say

"Game and software creation has never been easier or quicker than with Clickteam Fusion 2.5!

With Fusion 2.5's amazing event editor system you are able to quickly generate games or apps.

Within your first hour you will have learned the basics of the tool. Compile a windows app with a mouse click, or target additional platforms like iOS, Android, Flash and XNA (Windows Mobile phone and Xbox) with the purchase of our optional exporters. Harness the power of Clickteam Fusion 2.5 today."

Platforms

Windows, iOS, Android (including OUYA), XNA, Flash, HTML5

Purchase Options

Free Edition—a cut-down version, lacking many of the more powerful features.

Standard Edition—the Standard Edition has certain limitations compared to the Developer Edition. Includes the functionality to export to Windows and HTML5.

Developer Edition—same export formats as Standard, but without any restrictions.

Additional modules must be purchased to export to iOS, Android or Flash.

Developer

Clickteam

http://www.clickteam.com/multimedia-fusion-2

Example Games

- ► Really Big Sky
- ► Dungeon Dashers
- ► Six O'Clock High
- ► Odd Planet
- ► Neva
- ► Knytt Underground
- ► Legend of Princess
- ► Oniken
- ► GunGirl 2
- ► Spud's Quest
- ► Night Sky

Pros

- ► Good support for 2D games.
- ► Good solution for rapid prototyping of concepts.
- ► A code-less approach to development, so good for beginners.

Cons

- ► Not really suitable for complex games.
- ► More expensive than some of the other, similar, development kits.
- ► There can be performance issues when things get busy on-screen.

Game Salad

What They Say

"The World's Fastest Game Creation Engine. Design Games for Free—No Coding Required! There's no faster or easier way to develop games than with GameSalad Creator. Its visual, drag and drop interface and complex behaviour library provide almost limitless freedom to game designers. Bring your work to life in hours and days instead of weeks and months. It's all capable with GameSalad Creator!"

Platforms

Windows 8, Mac, iOS, Android

Purchase Options

The Free Edition allows you to publish on Mac and iOS, while the Pro Edition, which costs $300 per year, also includes Android and Windows 8 publishing and the following additional features—Twitter TweetSheet, Game Center, In-App Purchase, External Links and iAds.

Developer

GameSalad

http://gamesalad.com

Example Games

- SuperGolf
- CheeseMan
- Zombie Drop
- Help Volty
- Puck It
- Gravonaut
- Hobo with a Shotgun
- The Secret of Grisly Manor
- Bumps
- E-Pig Dash

Pros

- A nice seamless process for preparing everything you need for App Store (Mac and iOS) submissions.
- Many of the in-built tools and routines are nice and easy to use.
- Some very good docs and guides available on the GameSalad site.
- GameSalad Marketplace offers a wide range of pre-built game templates, art and audio assets—an excellent resource.

Cons

- GameSalad could certainly be described as a little quirky. I suspect that since the developers do not have a games background they tend to do things a little differently.
- Lack of regular updates and features—be wary of updates when they do arrive, as they are often known to break existing features.
- Not the best solution for performance on slower target platforms.

Another very useful GameSalad resource is DeepBlueApps (http://www.deepblueapps.com), who offer a wide range of different game templates and useful tools for GameSalad and Corona development.

App Game Kit

What They Say

"AGK was developed out of our own need to create a one stop solution for making game apps for mobile devices. In the past TGC had developed games for one device and then wanted to port them to other platforms. The process of conversion was costly and repetitive. The team wanted to spend more time creating new games and not burdened with laborious conversion work.

The TGC team has a wealth of experience in creating game creation tools spanning well over a decade. Taking that knowledge and working with our loyal and enthusiastic community we set to work on creating AGK.

This phase one of AGK is just the beginning. We aim to spread AGK across as many different platforms as possible. Meaning games you code in our AGK BASIC will instantly work on other supported platforms as we bring them into the AGK portfolio."

Platforms

Windows, Mac, iOS, Android, Blackberry

Purchase Options

There is a one-off fee of $59.99, with a planned price increase upon release of Version 2.

Developer

The Game Creators
http://www.appgamekit.com

Example Games

- ▶ Driving Test Success series
- ▶ Sky Without Sun: Target
- ▶ Space Connection: Atlas
- ▶ TRAX

Pros

- ▶ A good option for coding beginners as games and apps can be built in BASIC, which is a very straightforward language to learn.
- ▶ AGK also recently ran a successful Kickstarter campaign to help fund version 2, so development on that is now well under way with

planned support for extra drawing and sprite blending modes, shaders and enhanced 3D support.

▶ Very reasonably priced.

Cons

▶ Relatively unproven for commercial game releases.
▶ Not many built-in tools; you need to code most things in BASIC.
▶ Lack of regular updates.
▶ No asset store or online templates.

Marmalade

What They Say

"The Marmalade SDK enables developers to deploy code across multiple platforms and devices from a single code base in C++, Lua, HTML or Objective-C. In this section, we give you a high-level overview of the Marmalade platform, show you how it works and how you would use it, and provide details of the platforms that are supported.

There are four flavours of Marmalade:

▶ C++ for maximum cross-platform flexibility and performance
▶ Juice: Simplify porting of iOS apps and games to Android
▶ Quick Rapid 2D game development using Lua
▶ Web: Combine the power of C++ with HTML5"

Platforms

Windows, Mac, Linux, iOS, Android, Windows Phone 8, Tizen, Blackberry

Purchase Options

Community—supports iOS and Android

Indie—supports iOS, Android, Blackberry, Windows Phone 8

Plus—supports iOS, Android, Blackberry, Windows Phone 8, Mac, Windows, Connected TV

Professional—same platforms as Plus but you do not need to credit Marmalade in your app and you receive enhanced support

Developer

Ideaworks 3D
http://www.madewithmarmalade.com

Example Games

Some BIG names here:

- GODUS
- Cut the Rope
- Blur: Overdrive
- Mr Driller Aqua
- Draw Something
- Doodle Jump
- Need for Speed Shift
- Plants vs. Zombies
- Tetris
- Worms
- Monopoly
- Bejewelled Blitz
- Call of Duty Zombies
- The Sims 3
- Peggle
- Vector
- To-Fu 2
- City Conquest HD

Marmalade uses C++, so is a more traditional tool and a firm favourite with established game development studios and publishers such as EA, Team 17, Namco, Hotgen who most likely have existing code bases in C++.

In a move to appeal to smaller/less traditional developers, all Marmalade licences now include Marmalade Quick:

"As the name suggests, Marmalade Quick is designed to be fast, flexible and easy to use. With Marmalade Quick, a little code goes a long way. Using Lua (the fastest scripting language available), Marmalade Quick is built on Marmalade and Cocos2D-X so it is also powerful and entirely cross-platform. In fact, no other RAD environment offers simultaneous deployment to so many platforms—or the ability to develop for Android on a Mac and for iOS on a PC."

Pros

- Marmalade uses C++, which can be good for existing developers with C++ code bases.
- Traditional approach will certainly appeal to veteran game coders.

Cons

▶ Very high cost for commercial usage, I would find it hard to recommend Marmalade for this reason.

▶ Old-school approach to development.

▶ Definitely not a choice for beginners.

Cocos2d-x

What They Say

"Cocos2d-x is an open source game framework written in C++, with a thin platform dependent layer. It can be used to build games, apps and other cross platform GUI based interactive programs.

Brand New Graphic Renderer: The Cocos2d-x renderer is optimized for 2D graphics with OpenGL. It supports Skeletal Animation, Sprite Sheet Animation, Coordinate systems, Effects, multi resolution devices, Textures, Transitions, TileMaps and Particles. It adopts a RenderQueue design.

Cocos Studio is a free and professional game development toolkit that enables game developers to quickly create game content, and takes that tedious work and simplifies it with straightforward GUI editors.

Cocos Studio includes 4 core game development editors: UI Editor, Animation Editor, Scene Editor and Data Editor. Developers can focus on their specific roles and enjoy better streamlined workflow. This enables game studios to collaborate with ease, and focus on what each does best in order to achieve better quality and faster turnaround time. This saves time and money."

Platforms

iOS, Android, Blackberry, Windows Phone, Tizen, HTML5

Purchase Options

Cocos2D-x is free under an open source MIT licence.

Developer

Various

http://www.cocos2D-x.org

Example Games

Worldwide, more than 400,000 developers, including developers of 7 out of the 10 top grossing games in China, rely on Cocos2D-x to build their mobile games. Here are a few:

▶ Diamond Dash
▶ City of Wonder
▶ Zenonia 5
▶ Farmville
▶ Matching with Friends
▶ Small City
▶ Super Stick Golf 2
▶ Contra: Evolution
▶ Raiden Legacy
▶ TouchMix 2

Pros

▶ Cocos is supported by a number of excellent (and free) third-party apps, which cover 2D level creation (including the excellent 'Tiled' Map Editor), particle effects, bitmap font usage and rapid development tools such as CocosBuilder and CocoMoon Studio.
▶ With Javascript, Lua and C++ support, a wide range of supported platforms and a solid selection of tools, it is hard not to recommend Cocos.
▶ Best of all, it is completely free. You really can't ask for more than that!
▶ Massive support community.

Cons

▶ Not as easy to learn as some of the other development kits.

Corona

What They Say

"Corona's extensive API library enables everything, from animation to networking, with a few lines of code. Whether you're building games or business apps, you see changes instantly in the Corona Simulator and can iterate extremely quickly. Development is done in Lua, a lightning-fast, easy to learn scripting language.

Corona SDK allows you to publish for iOS, Android, Kindle Fire and NOOK from a single code base. And Windows Phone 8 and Windows 8 are coming soon!

We'll take care of the heavy lifting related to device and platform fragmentation, allowing you to focus on creating exceptional mobile content."

Platforms
iOS, Android

Purchase Options
Corona SDK Basic is a lower cost solution that allows you to build and publish your apps to the app stores, currently costing just under $200 per year.

Corona SDK Pro (approx. $600 per year) adds advanced graphics, all Corona Plugins, analytics and much more.

Corona SDK Enterprise—expensive! Call any native library (C++/ Objective-C/Java) from your Corona app and do offline builds. Unlikely you will need this initially.

Developer
Corona Labs
http://www.coronalabs.com/

Example Games
- ► Throne Wars
- ► Major Magnet
- ► Fun Run
- ► Blast Monkeys
- ► Mandora
- ► Sushi Friends
- ► Hello Kitty Happy Town
- ► ShaqDown
- ► Ocean Tower

Pros
- ► A solid 2D solution.
- ► Relatively easy to develop for.
- ► Support for hardware Accelerometer, GPS, Compass, camera etc.

Cons

► Only supports a limited number of target platforms.
► The licence fees are steep, particularly for the Enterprise solutions, and I am not keen on the way the website quotes licences as a monthly fee when in fact they are single, annual payments.
► Corona can be very slow at implementing new features.
► Apparently the Android support can be buggy.

Insider Indie Q&A

1. What is the name of your studio?

Glitch Games

© Glitch Games

2. What year was your studio founded and what are the names of the founders?

2012 by Graham Ranson and Simon Pearce

3. What are the studio's key game titles?

Our main series is our Forever Lost adventure series—www.foreverlostgame.com

4. Do you have your own in-house engine or use a third party system? If third party, which one do you use?

We use the Corona SDK from Corona Labs—www.coronalabs.com—but then have our own in-house adventure game framework on top of that called Serenity.

5. Which platforms do you release on now / plan to release on?

Currently we can only release on iOS and Android (both Google Play and Amazon) as that is what the Corona SDK supports. Mac App Store, Windows App Store, Windows Phone 8 and Web release support are currently in Beta so we hope to be able to release on those platforms very soon.

6. *Which is your most successful platform so far?*

    Currently it is iOS.

7. *What are the development tools you use most (i.e. 2D, 3D software, audio tools etc.)?*

    For the code side I use Sublime Text for development and naturally the Corona SDK. When we dip into audio we use Audacity. For the art side it is Photoshop and a 3D modelling suite, I honestly can't remember which one though, I'd have to ask Simon.

8. *What advice would you give to a new studio?*

    Find a niche audience and stick to it, make the best games you can in that niche and create a name for yourself. It's much easier to market to a niche without the budget of the big guys, which will allow your studio to do the single most important thing, survive.

9. *What marketing resources do you use?*

    Twitter/Facebook and a newsletter.

10. *What are your favourite indie games sites?*

    We read a lot of PocketGamer in the office, as well as the other usual suspects like IndieStatik, IndieHaven, TouchArcade, IndieGames.com, Jayls-Games and a few others I feel bad for forgetting.

11. *Any mistakes/hiccups you have made so far, something you would advise a new studio to avoid?*

    Don't bite off more than you can chew with your first game and set your expectations much lower for it. Get ready to fail a lot.

Flash

What They Say

"Adobe® Flash® Builder® 4.7 software is a development environment for building games and applications using the ActionScript® language and the open source Flex framework. Flash Builder Premium includes professional testing tools such as profilers, network monitoring and unit testing support."

Adobe also supply a dedicated gaming SDK to accompany Flash Builder, called the Adobe Gaming SDK: "The Adobe Gaming SDK provides an essential collection of frameworks, code samples and learning resources that work together to help developers create and deliver ActionScript games across multiple devices."

You also have access to the Native extensions, which let you take advantage of platform-specific capabilities on iOS, Android, Windows and Mac. Want to go 3D? Stage3D allows you to use hardware accelerated graphics in your games.

Last, but not least, Adobe provide a very comprehensive profiling system, called Scout. Adobe Scout is the next-generation profiling tool for Adobe Flash Player and AIR.

Platforms

Flash games can run on a large number of platforms as stand-alone apps, or via a web browser. This includes all major mobile platforms, including iOS and Android.

Purchase Options

Flash and Flash Builder are now part of Adobe Creative Cloud, which allows you to download and use every Adobe program for a monthly licence fee.

Developer

Adobe
http://www.adobe.com

Example Games

- ► Canabalt
- ► Ruby Blast Adventures
- ► Angry Birds
- ► Help Me Fly
- ► Snailboy
- ► CSI: Miami Heat Wave
- ► Roller Coaster Mania
- ► Swerve
- ► Super Puzzle Platformer
- ► Kung Fu Attack
- ► Super Gem Heroes

In addition to the Adobe supplied tools, there are several other solutions out there for Flash development, all designed specifically for games with a number of powerful features including split screen support, bitmap fonts, blending modes, tile editors, animation, sprite sheets, tweening, replays, physics, particles, game saves and more. All are available on an open source licence, and have very active communities:

Starling
Website: http://gamua.com/starling/

"Starling does not cost a dime. Download and use it right away—no strings attached. And because it is open source, you're always in control: step through the code and learn from its internals. Everything is well documented and easy to understand. Drop your in-house engine and focus on your games!"

Flixel
Website: http://flixel.org/index.html

Flixel is an open source game-making library that is completely free for personal or commercial use. Written entirely in Actionscript 3, and designed to be used with free development tools, Flixel is easy to learn, extend and customize.

FlashPunk
Website: http://useflashpunk.net/

FlashPunk is a free ActionScript 3 library designed for developing 2D Flash games. It provides you with a fast, clean framework to prototype and develop your games in. This means that most of the dirty work is already done, letting you concentrate on the design and testing of your game.

Pros
▶ A low-cost and incredibly powerful and flexible system.
▶ The internet is awash with great Flash creation tutorials, templates and code examples.
▶ Some amazing third-party tools and game engine extensions available, all for free!
▶ Proven 'in the field' for many years; performance is good.

Cons
▶ It's Flash! You either love it or hate it.
▶ Complexity—can be rather daunting for beginners.
▶ Support for some platforms is not as straightforward as with other development kits.

Insider Indie Q&A

1. *What is the name of your studio?*

   nDreams

   # n Dreams

2. *What year was your studio founded and what are the names of the founders?*

   2006, Patrick O'Luanaigh

3. *What are the studio's key game titles?*

   Xi/Aurora (PlayStation Home), Secret Life (web ARG), SkyDIEving (Oculus Rift)

4. *Do you have your own in-house engine or use a third party system? If third party, which one do you use?*

   We use Unity.

5. *Which platforms do you release on now / plan to release on?*

   Mainly PlayStation Home so far, but a few mobile titles coming, and console/PR

6. *Which is your most successful platform so far?*

   PlayStation Home—we've become one of the leading global publishers.

7. *What are the development tools you use most (i.e. 2D, 3D software, audio tools etc.)?*

   Autodesk Maya, ZBrush, Photoshop, Unity

8. *What advice would you give to a new studio?*

   Don't be afraid to form relationships with other companies—don't try to do everything yourselves!

9. *What marketing resources do you use?*

   We have an in-house marketing person, and outside of PlayStation Home, we're working with co-publishing partners.

10. *What are your favourite indie games sites?*

    Don't have one—tend to use social media!

11. *Any mistakes/hiccups you have made so far, something you would advise a new studio to avoid?*

    Track cash flow, don't assume you're going to have a hit, and network a lot.

Art and Design Resources

During the course of development, more often than not I have had fairly limited financial budgets to work with. As such, I have used pre-built art resources extensively. Several sites offer high-quality collections of 3D models, animations, 2D artwork, sprite animations and textures that are usually very reasonably priced.

Often you can save many months of work by carefully sourcing pre-created collections, and with a little tweaking and re-texturing here and there you can really make such art your own and tailor it to your game.

As an example, you may buy a pack of skyscraper meshes but re-texture many of the surfaces (again using bought in assets). Add your own signage and props, and with fairly minimal time and effort you have something unique for your game. Compare that to recruiting an artist, who could take several weeks to achieve the same results if creating the artwork from scratch.

Below I have included a list and summary of several of the places I have used in the past, so all of these come with a personal recommendation.

Turbosquid
Website: http://www.turbosquid.com/

The biggest collection of art resources on the internet; there is an absolute treasure trove of content on here and it has a very good navigation interface. You do have to be careful with the quality and polygon count for some assets, but I have found the quality to be mostly pretty good with plenty of outstandingly good models. There are also hundreds of game ready, low polygon models with normal mapped textures (just type 'game ready' in the search engine to view them).

Dexsoft
Website: http://www.3dmodels-textures.com/store/

Very high-quality meshes and textures, all of which are game ready. They have a number of different theme types, including sci-fi, modern day, fantasy, vegetation and 3D characters. The prices are very competitive too, so it is a great resource. One thing to be aware of—some of the models can be a little high poly, so make sure you check the PDF details for each collection to ensure the poly counts match with your requirements before you buy. I would say Dexsoft collections are mostly tailored to PC/console type games rather than lower spec mobile devices.

Game Textures
Website: https://gametextures.com/

One of the newest texture sites, and one of the best. A nice range of architectural, sci-fi and natural textures, all of which feature a full range of maps including normal, specular, height and emissive. The textures on Game Textures are modern 'AAA' quality, low cost and rather wonderful.

GameDev Market
Website: https://www.gamedevmarket.net

GameDev Market is a new entry in the field, current at beta phase. There are quite a few good quality 3D and 2D assets on here. There are two types of licence for each asset, commercial and non-commercial, with the commercial licence costing more.

Marlin Studios
Website: http://www.marlinstudios.com/

I have only used their texture collections (they also do models), but these are a little dated now. Marlin haven't released any new content for several years, so their texture collections lack up-to-date features such as normal maps. Also, many of the textures are a little low-resolution, but that said they are still very good quality and ideal for mobile.

3DTotal Textures
Website: http://shop.3Dtotal.com/total-textures.html

A mixed bag of textures with some odd aspect ratios not ideally suited to games. The prices of the texture collections are relatively cheap and there are enough good textures to make the collections worth owning.

Absolute Textures
Website: http://www.absolutetextures.com/

Like Marlin Studios these are getting on in years now, so lacking essential features like normal maps. That said there are some good town and city architectural texture packs, but the prices are quite steep.

Sub Dimension Studios
Website: http://subdimensionstudios.com/

Some good textures, particularly the natural textures and architectural edging and tile textures. The prices are low, but again there are no normal maps.

Arroway Textures
Website: http://www.arroway-textures.com/

Collections of base building material textures such as wood, concrete, stonework and tiles. The textures are of a high standard and are very high resolution but often in sizes and aspect ratios that are not compatible with games, so you will need to do some work to make usable textures.

CG Textures
Website: http://www.cgtextures.com/

A huge range of photo textures, most optimized for game use (the site founder has a background in games). Just about everyone in 'the biz' uses CG Textures, and the subscription prices are low and provide unlimited access for a year.

Human Photo References
Website: http://www.3D.sk/

A great site that specializes in human reference textures such as skin, eyes and pre-made head textures.

Backyard Ninja Free Stuff
Website: http://www.dumbmanex.com/bynd_freestuff.html

A small selection of free to use pixel/2D art. A mixed bag but certainly some good examples on here.

OpenGameArt
Website: http://opengameart.org/

A great selection of free 2D, 3D and sound resources. Quality varies from awful to great, but there are plenty of gems on here. Be sure to read the usage licence for each item before you use. While many are free to use, other content is covered by rather silly restrictive licences, which makes commercial use impossible.

Graphic River/Envato Network
Website: http://graphicriver.net/

I love this site—if you want 2D and vector art, this is the place to go. But why stop there? They also have dedicated sites that sell 3D art, sound effect, video clips, code and stock photos. One of the best resources for developers on the internet.

Graphic River has also recently added a number of 2D game tile sets, sprites, GUIs and other game-specific content.

Audio Resources

Need some quality sound effects or music? If you want to keep your costs down I can recommend having a look through these sites. Again, be sure to read and understand the usage licences for any free content.

FreeSound.org
Website: http://www.freesound.org/

Freesound aims to create a huge collaborative database of audio snippets, samples, recordings, and bleeps released under Creative Commons licences that allow their reuse.

Audio Jungle
Website: http://audiojungle.net/

135,266 royalty-free audio files from $1. Music loops, music packs, sound effects, source files, logos and idents.

DigCCMixter
Website: http://dig.ccmixter.org/

This site includes a small 'free music for commercial projects' section, under an attribution licence.

Flash Kit
Website: http://www.flashkit.com/soundfx/

Offers an ever-growing list of shareware and freeware Sound FX for download.

Free Music Archive
Website: http://freemusicarchive.org/

It's not just free music; it's good music.

Indie Game Music
Website: http://www.indiegamemusic.com/

You can find music for various platforms; MIDI for e.g. Java ME, MODs; XMs for e.g. Gamepark/PSP/Nintendo DS; S3Ms for e.g. Gameboy Advance; MP3s for e.g. Flash.

Lucky Lion Studios
Website: http://luckylionstudios.com/

Lucky Lion Studios provides high-quality video game music at an affordable price, whether you're an independent developer in need of a few select songs or an established studio seeking an entire original score.

Partners in Rhyme
Website: http://www.partnersinrhyme.com/pir/PIRsfx.shtml

Free sound effects and royalty-free sound effects.

Sound Bible
Website: http://soundbible.com/

Free sound clips, sound bites and sound effects.

Sound Jay
Website: http://www.soundjay.com/

Another free sound effects website. Most files are 16 bit stereo 44.1 kHz or 48 kHz high-quality sound effects (i.e. ideal for games).

Sample Swap
Website: http://sampleswap.org/

Professional quality, free audio samples and electronic music.

Sound Dogs
Website: http://www.sounddogs.com/sound-effects.asp

The world's first online commercial sound effects and production music library. Offers a large, easily accessible sound library for immediate download (in .aiff, .wav. and .mp3) and the packaged (on CD/DVD or hard drive) 'Soundstorm' library.

Shockwave Sound
Website: http://www.shockwave-sound.com/

One of the pioneers of online royalty-free music, stock music and downloadable sound effect libraries. I've used Shockwave Sound quite a bit in the past, and the quality can be very good.

Insider Indie Q&A

1. What is the name of your studio?

Total Monkery

2. What year was your studio founded and what are the names of the founders?

Founded in 2012 by Richard Weeks and Andrea Chadler.

3. *What are the studio's key game titles?*

Magnets is our current game which will be out in October. I have worked in games for over 20 years, though this is just the first time I've made things for myself.

4. *Do you have your own in-house engine or use a third party system? If third party, which one do you use?*

Everyone uses Unity Pro. We have some things that still work in XNA, but we have migrated over the last 18 months.

5. *Which platforms do you release on now / plan to release on?*

Magnets will be released on PC, Mac and Linux. Once those are out we will port it to work on WiiU, PS4, XBone, 3DS and Vita. We have Nintendo dev. status; the others are in the pipe. We will look at mobile later as we feel entering that market requires some weight behind you (which helps if you have a successful game already).

6. *Which is your most successful platform so far?*

We don't have a product out yet. From some market research we did, it looks like Steam is the clear favourite but whether that turns into actual extra sales, we don't know.

7. *What are the development tools you use most (i.e. 2D, 3D software, audio tools etc.)?*

Blender, Photoshop, Illustrator, After Effects, NDO, XNView, Audacity, Visual Studio, Tortoise SVN, Fraps.

8. *What advice would you give to a new studio?*

Make a business plan and be realistic about what you want to make. Start off doing something manageable and that you have sufficient funds for. Things will come along to throw you off course, make sure you can ride out those problems.

9. *What marketing resources do you use?*

We started with PR help and used it until funds for it ran out. We actively use Twitter and engage with IndieDB as much as possible. We read as many articles as we can on the games industry and "data mine" them to give us ideas about where we should focus. We do the same with YouTubers and previewers. Work out who would be more applicable to us and try them first.

10. *What are your favourite indie games sites?*

IndieDB, Rock Paper Shotgun, IndieGames, IndieGameMag.

11. *Any mistakes/hiccups you have made so far, something you would advise a new studio to avoid?*

Not having a good business plan from the beginning and staying focused on one product. We worked on multiple titles before settling on Magnets as we had to react to where funding was available. If we were sensible at the beginning we would have probably waited until we had more money before starting up.

Outsourcing

Another option to consider, and this can work in conjunction with using pre-built assets, is to outsource art, code or music. This is a step toward building up a development team, but reduces many of the additional costs and risks inherent with employing staff.

Although there can be many different types of agreements, in general you outsource a specific task or chunk of the project, agree on a fee and get started. As such, you only pay when you need actual work, and it can be a very convenient, flexible and cash-flow friendly way of working. You can swiftly ramp up resources on a project by hiring simultaneous artists, musicians etc. to create your assets. By way of an example, one of our games required several different music tracks—nine in total, in a very short time frame. Rather than trying to get one musician to create all the tunes, we hired five different musicians, at pretty much the same time to write the tracks. The tracks were all done within a few days, and actually we were able to keep the costs down as we set a specific fee for each tune. This cost less than if we had commissioned one musician to do x minutes of music.

Another approach you can use for outsourcing is to agree to a split between revenue share and fee-based work, or even go full revenue share. Many indie studios often have almost no cash reserves or cash flow while developing a game; revenue share may be the only way such a studio can afford to develop their game. You will have to go to some lengths to convince a contractor to work with you on those terms, though, so you'll need a solid and realistic game proposal, time frame and marketing plan in place. I have included an interview with a freelance artist below, which highlights some of these issues.

Typically a revenue share deal works as follows: you agree to a percentage of the sales revenue for the game, which is split as soon as the money comes in; that is, no costs are taken off beforehand, just a split off the top. This can also work well for all parties, as everyone then has a vested interest in the project and gets to share in the reward if the game is successful.

Another positive for outsourcing is that you don't have to buy equipment (e.g. workstations, software), as contractors will usually have all their own facilities. You can build up a team, with no initial set-up costs, which is a very indie-friendly way of working.

So, where can you go to find outsource contractors? We have used several different sites in the past to advertise for contractors, and this has always worked out well, with plenty of high-quality applicants. You do, of course, get some poor ones, but if you carefully check portfolios and ask the right questions, you can soon separate the good from the bad. So, let's look at the sites to try . . .

deviantART
Website: http://www.deviantart.com

Every type of artist you could ever need can be found on deviantART—3D, 2D, pixel, illustrators, texture artists and so on. You can search for the type of art you need, check the online examples then fire them a message.

Pixel Joint
Website: http://www.pixeljoint.com

If you need high-quality 2D pixel art, Pixel Joint is the place. You can search the galleries for examples that match the style you need, and then contact the artist directly. You can also post on the forums and advertise the job, and wait for applicants to come to you. This can be the best approach, as many of the gallery artists may not be available at the specific time that you need.

Way of the Pixel
Website: http://wayofthepixel.net/

Way of the Pixel is a discussion forum for pixel artists; as such, it is a great place to post job ads and you will usually see a very good response.

GameArtisans
Website: http://www.gameartisans.org/forums/forum.php

GameArtisans is a site where game artists showcase their work, with a focus on 3D and concept art. The quality of artwork is very high, and you can browse the artist portfolios easily—you can be sure that it won't take long to find a top-notch artist. You can also advertise specific jobs on the site.

TIGForums
Website: http://forums.tigsource.com

TIGForums is a great place to find contractors for all disciplines, and one I have found to be very successful in the past. In addition to artists and musicians showing off their portfolios, you can post jobs on the forums, and the responses are usually very good.

IndieGamer Forums
Website: http://forums.indiegamer.com

Very similar to the TIGForums, IndieGamer Forums is a site that I have found to work well in the past when I have advertised for contractors. Again, it covers all disciplines.

ChipMusic.org
Website: http://chipmusic.org

This is a brilliant site to find top quality artists—musicians with an electronic leaning. Again, this is forum based; you post a job and wait for the replies. I have always received plenty of replies, and have found every musician I have worked with through this site.

Outsourcing Agreements

When outsourcing the development of your indie game to remote workers, make sure you put together an agreement from the outset.

You need to specify exactly what your requirements are, the payment terms, the deliverable dates and all other aspects.

Possibly the most important point is the copyright assignment—you must get full assignment of the copyright from the contractor. If you don't do this, it can and most likely will come back to bite you in the butt—especially if there is a dispute later in the project.

Clear expectations for both sides are necessary to ensure smooth running of the development. Do you have a certain time frame you need the work completed in? If so, specify it clearly. You can even add penalty clauses if the deadline is very important. For example, if you are developing a game for a third party and they need it by a specific date, you can stipulate that the contractor will lose a percentage of the fee if they miss the deadline.

You must ensure that you clearly detail the nature of the work and the required deliverables. If you need artwork in a specific file format or code in a particular language, then write it down. Don't leave any ambiguity; be as specific as possible.

Both sides must be very clear on how much and when the contractor will be paid, and this should be tied to the deliverable dates. Never agree to an hourly rate or an open-ended payment structure; if you do, you could get your fingers burned and get badly overcharged. Agree to a specific fee for the work, and all sides will know what is expected from the start—no nasty surprises.

Ensure you include a termination clause. After all, not all projects work out well, and you need to be covered for such eventualities. Detail the grounds for termination. For example, if the contractor's work is unsatisfactory, then you need to state in your agreement that they can be removed from the project without further obligation.

Last, make sure you have a non-disclosure clause, to avoid sensitive information about the game being leaked when you don't want it to be.

I have just completed a major game update on our PC/Mac title, Life of Pixel, with an art contractor named Danny Flexner. It was a very enjoyable and rewarding experience, and I thought it would be good to chat with Danny to get a contractor's perspective on how a good outsourcing agreement should work. So, over to Danny . . .

Outsourcing Notes From a Freelancer Perspective

Initial Contact

The first contact between a potential client and a freelancer can be critical, just like any business interaction. Whenever I send emails out to companies or indies that I want to do work for, I'll try to keep it brief and include my current resume and a portfolio that's tailored for whatever their job posting was (if they're only looking for animators, then it doesn't make sense to include background work). I give them a short introduction about who I am and explain that I'm interested in helping them with their project and that I'd like to know more about it if they're interested in working with me.

What I Look for in a Studio

If you've been freelancing long enough and have an effective business presence on the web, then sometimes indie developers will contact you. Obviously, this gives you a little leverage, since your work has already made a positive impression and people are interested in working with you. At this point, it's up to the potential client to convince you that their project is worth your time.

I get approached by indies often enough to recognize red flags quickly. These include:

▶ Being asked to work on a large project that will only pay in revenue shares at the end. A lot of new indie developers will try to make something big like an RPG as their first project, only to completely miscalculate how long it will take to finish the project. This is a big warning sign of poor planning.

▶ Being asked to do work for free, or "for your portfolio" is a warning sign. If a potential client is contacting you in the first place, then you've already got a good portfolio and you don't need their project to make it better. These are the kind of clients who would love to take advantage of a freelancer's willingness to do work and quickly pile on more "little" requests.

▶ Being asked to work on a project, and the client discusses money right away. No one should start talking about money in the first emails; this should come once the freelancer knows all the details and is asked to make a quote, or the freelancer asks about the budget and timeline after knowing the details.

▶ Being asked to work on a new project, but the developer doesn't have a game design document in place. If you ask to see the game design document, and the response is, "I have it in my head," that's a problem. This means that the whole team can't be on the same page about what's going on with the game and that there probably isn't a clear vision of what the game is. Again, it's a sign of poor planning.

It essentially comes down to this: can the client pay you adequately for the work they want done, and have they planned out their project? If so, then it's probably worth doing the project. If not, then working on that project is a big risk with low odds of a good payout for you.

My general advice to any studio looking for a freelance artist: don't reach out until you have the pre-production phase of the project done.

Working Relationship and Contact

As an independent contractor, the relationship you have with your clients is important to your business model. Most of the work successful freelancers do isn't done for new clients; it's for returning clients. Having a good relationship with your clients means that you'll be on their shortlist when they need more work for other projects.

It's also good to maintain a consistent pace of contact with your client. You don't always have to respond instantly to emails, but trying to respond within the day you get them is good practice. Vanishing for days at a time in the middle of a project can be frustrating and throw development off for the rest of the team. If you know you're not going to be available during certain days or times, then it's a good idea to give the client a heads up if you're in the middle of developing a project.

In general, it's good to keep things professional too. Even if you've worked with a client for several years, the way you interact with them and what you expect of them (and what they should expect of you) shouldn't be any different than a new client.

What Appeals to You When Working on a Project?

There are three reasons why artists work on a project: fame, fun and fortune. In my case, since I freelance for a living, money always needs to be a part of the reason I work on a project.

I'll also ask myself, "Will this project be good in my portfolio?" It's never the sole reason I'll work on a project, but any work I take on needs to be good enough to be in my portfolio. It can at least be a bright side to the project if the budget isn't quite where I'd like it to be. After all, as a freelancer, your income depends on your portfolio.

Just as an aside, usually you'll need to transfer over the rights to the work you complete to the client/company, and that's fine. But it's important to make sure you have a contract that specifically says that you can put the work you did for them in your portfolio afterward. Legally you want to have that language clearly stated; otherwise some people will actually try to stop you from displaying the work you created (for a number of reasons).

There have also been times where I just don't like the concept of a project enough to want to work on it. Maybe their budget was "ok" and it would have been "ok" in my portfolio, but I just hated the subject matter or concept. I wouldn't have fun working on it, or it just had themes that I fundamentally disagreed with.

Other than the "core" reasons for working on a particular project, seeing a clearly planned out project also appeals to me. If I can look over a game design document and see that it's clearly planned out, then I can do my job better. I can give better time and cost estimates, think about the work in advance and generally just make better art, because I can see how everything is connected.

Development Tools and Resources

Microsoft BizSpark

If you are a start-up studio (less than three years old) I recommend you join the Microsoft BizSpark program. As well as a lot of help and support and networking opportunities, it gives you free access to all Microsoft software (incredible but true).

Below are a few details from the BizSpark website—and considering there is no charge at all for joining, this really is the best offer around for start-ups.

Website: http://www.microsoft.com/bizspark/default.aspx

Program Overview

The Microsoft BizSpark program is based on the belief that start-up success is our success. Microsoft is committed to helping technology start-ups realize their goals on their own terms and in the shortest amount of time. Through BizSpark, Microsoft's goals are to:

Help young and innovative software companies gain valuable experience and expertise in Microsoft technologies, with no upfront costs.

Help start-ups establish connections with local and global start-up ecosystems—VCs, angels, incubators, entrepreneur associations etc.

Stimulate vibrant local software ecosystems and promote innovation and interoperability.

Support the broadest possible start-up audience in a way that complements their values and the organizations that support them.

Software

Access to 900+ current, full-featured software development tools, platform technologies and server products to build software applications. BizSpark start-ups also get free monthly Windows Azure benefits enabling them to quickly build, deploy and manage Web applications.

Support

Start-ups become part of the BizSpark ecosystem and get access to investors and advisors and valuable offers to help run their businesses, find talent and obtain financing. Start-ups also get access to technical, product and business training and support.

Eligibility

Eligible start-ups must be:

Actively engaged in development of a software-based product or service that will form a core piece of its current or intended business.

To meet this requirement the software must:
- ▶ add significant and primary functionality to the integrated Microsoft software;
- ▶ be owned, not licenced by the start-up;
- ▶ be privately held;
- ▶ have been in business for less than five years and
- ▶ bring in less than US$1 million in annual revenue.

Adobe Creative Cloud

I always considered owning a full suite of Adobe products a bit of a dream, given that each one costs several hundred dollars. Well Uncle Adobe has made my dream a reality by introducing the Creative Cloud program. For a monthly fee, you now have full access to everything Adobe develops, which really is a no-brainer for any serious game developer.

What They Say

"Your favourite tools are about to get even better. Introducing Creative Cloud™ desktop applications, including Adobe® Photoshop® CC and Illustrator® CC. They're the next generation of CS tools. Get hundreds of all-new features. New ways to keep your creative world in sync—feature updates, settings, and feedback from team members. And, as always, your applications live on your desktop, not in a browser and not in the cloud."

Software

The following packages are all included with Creative Cloud:

- Photoshop® CC (Image editing and compositing)
- Illustrator® CC (Vector graphics and illustration)
- InDesign® CC (Page design, layout and publishing)
- Dreamweaver® CC (Websites, app design and coding)
- After Effects® CC (Cinematic visual effects and motion graphics)
- Adobe® Premiere® Pro CC (Video production and editing)
- Adobe Muse™ CC (Website design without coding)
- Acrobat® XI Pro
- Adobe Audition® CC
- Bridge CC
- Encore®
- Fireworks®
- Flash® Builder® Premium
- Flash Professional CC
- InCopy® CC
- Lightroom®
- Media Encoder CC
- Prelude® CC
- SpeedGrade® CC

Insider Indie Q&A

1. *What is the name of your studio?*

Beatshapers Limited

2. *What year was your studio founded and what are the names of the founders?*

Domain registered back in 2006 but fully operation it's become in 2009.

I'm only the founder, Alexey Menshikov.

3. *What are the studio's key game titles?*

By November 2013, we released 18 titles across PlayStation® platforms.

They are ports mostly, but our own titles are BreakQuest: Extra Evolution, PS Vita launch StarDrone Extreme and Zrun (PS Vita).

4. *Do you have your own in-house engine or use a third party system? If third party, which one do you use?*

We have two pipelines: for one we have an in-house engine and for the PS4 title we licensed BitSquid Tech.

5. *Which platforms do you release on now / plan to release on?*

We are licensed for all platforms, but our plans are for PS4 and Xbox One and PC. Also tables.

6. *Which is your most successful platform so far?*

For now, it's PSP.

7. *What are the development tools you use most (i.e. 2D, 3D software, audio tools etc.)?*

Too many of them to list! The more unique ones are Pacarana for sound design and some texture generation tools.

8. *What advice would you give to a new studio?*

Don't clone: invent, mix and experiment a lot.

9. *What marketing resources do you use?*

Over the past four years of operation, we have compiled a large mailing list of journalists. Sometimes we are active on NeoGaf and other forums and use our friends at http://game-newswire.com/.

10. *What are your favourite indie game sites?*

Indie Games Mag, I think. I'm reading some Russian language sites and blogs.

Actually, my Facebook friends deliver a lot of news daily.

11. *Any mistakes/hiccups you have made so far, something you would advise a new studio to avoid?*

We started our company from porting titles from one format to another because we weren't backed by any investors etc., and we needed a cash flow. This type of work, however, adds little value to a company.

If I started now, I'd make a few experimental games instead.

Don't invent technology unless you need a really special one.

My Software Kit List

There are hundreds of amazing packages out there, so rather than trying to list them all, I will cover the packages I use regularly. As with many other indie developers, I favour lower cost/free options. The good news is that these are incredibly good packages, and in many cases they are better than more expensive alternatives.

Tiled
Website: http://www.mapeditor.org/

The best tile editor out there—so far I have used this to create the levels in two games: Life of Pixel and SuperGolf. It is a breeze to use and incredibly powerful. Supports orthogonal, isometric and staggered maps.

Explosion Generator 3
Website: http://www.deepblueapps.com/explosion-generator-3/

An amazingly useful tool that creates 2D sprite-sheets or individual frame explosion animations, blood splats, exploding objects and more.

BMFont
Website: http://www.angelcode.com/products/bmfont/

A basic tool for creating bitmap font sheets. It does the job, but there is no finesse, so a better choice is . . .

Glyph Designer
Website: http://www.71squared.com/en/glyphdesigner

Now this is more like it. Bitmap font creation with love; supports shadows, gradient fills, strokes and more. Mac only is the only downside.

Particle Designer
Website: http://www.71squared.com/en/particledesigner

A very powerful and well-featured particle creation system which outputs to a number of different game frameworks including Cocos, Kobold2D, Moai, Starling, Pixelwave, NME, Marmalade and Platino.

TimelineFX
Website: http://www.rigzsoft.co.uk/

Another particle animation creation tool that gives amazingly good
results. I used Timeline extensively for sprite sheet explosions and
effects in our PSM game MegaBlast and it worked a treat.

FRAPS
Website: http://www.fraps.com

FRAPS is a great tool to use to record screenshots and video game
footage directly from a PC game. It is very reliable and does the job well,
every time.

Shader Map 2
Website: http://shadermap.com/home/

A brilliant tool for creating normal, specular and height maps from
photo textures. I used this extensively for creating normal maps in our
Vita debut title Indoor Sports World.

Large 3D Terrain Generator (L3DT)
Website: http://www.bundysoft.com/L3DT/

Designed specifically for games, this terrain editor generates
editable-height maps where you can specify land altitudes, roughness,
lakes, climate, etc. It also supports the creation and export of terrain
textures, light maps, bump maps and alpha/splat maps.

Google Sketchup
Website: http://www.sketchup.com/

Sketchup comes in two flavours, the free 'Make' and the $590 'Pro'
edition. I'd ignore the Pro version and use Make—then go onto the
3D Warehouse and smile. Thousands of free 3D models that can be
downloaded and adapted to use in your games.

ProMotion
Website: http://www.cosmigo.com/promotion/index.php

The best pixel editor out there. ProMotion includes everything you will ever need for drawing and animating pixel sprites, backgrounds and tiles.

ACDSee
Website: http://www.acdsee.com/

I use ACDSee for browsing images on my PC. I have thousands of textures, bitmaps and whatnot, so this is an invaluable tool. You can also batch edit and process images; ideal for converting batches of images to different file formats.

Inkscape
Website: http://inkscape.org/

I must confess I haven't used Inkscape; I have Adobe Illustrator as part of Creative Cloud. Inkscape however is very well regarded and apparently an excellent free tool for creating and editing vector images.

Aseprite
Website: http://www.aseprite.org/

Another high-quality 2D pixel art drawing tool, this has really good palette manipulation features.

Gimp
Website: http://www.gimp.org/

A free alternative to Adobe Photoshop. Jam-packed with features and well supported by the community.

Blender
Website: http://www.blender.org/

THE 3D package of choice when you are on a tight budget. It is free, yet does everything you will ever need. It even has its own built-in game engine, incredible stuff!

FLStudio
Website: http://www.image-line.com/documents/flstudio.html

FLStudio (formerly Fruity Loops) is a brilliant music creation package, which comes packed with a whole host of audio plugins and tools. FL Studio supports all PC industry plugin instrument standards including VST, DX, Buzz and Rewire.

Bfxr
Website: http://www.bfxr.net/

A great, and free, sound effects creation tool. You will hear sound effects in many indie games made with Bfxr.

Audacity
Website: http://audacity.sourceforge.net/

A free sound-sample editing package that will allow you to edit sound effects and apply filters. Essential for creating sounds for games.

SayIt
Website: http://www.analogx.com/contents/download/Audio/sayit/Freeware.htm

A free speech-synthesis program. Type in what you want to record, tweak the voice settings and output your WAV.

LabChirp
Website: http://labbed.net/software.php?id=labchirp

Another free sound-effect creation package. Offers a number of different options to Bfxr, so it is well worth installing both this and Bfxr.

Reaper
Website: http://www.cockos.com/reaper/

Reaper is another great music creation package (DAW). It is also the lowest priced option, offering excellent value for money.

Image Compression Tools

Many App Store and Google Play games feature high-quality screenshots that load almost instantly. Minimal waiting time for the potential customer, while maintaining perfect visual clarity. Why do they load so much quicker than my Photoshop PNGs?

Answer: clever image compression—and there are a number of good tools out there that are designed to minimise image size without compromising on image quality. Good news for cash flow too: these tools are all free to use.

Compressor.io
Website: https://compressor.io

Compressor.io is a powerful online tool for reducing drastically the size of your images and photos whilst maintaining a high quality with almost no difference before and after compression.

The following file formats are supported—JPEG, PNG, GIF and SVG, and there are two types of compression, lossless or lossy.

Smush.it
Website: http://www.smushit.com/ysmush.it/

Smush.it uses optimization techniques specific to image format to remove unnecessary bytes from image files. It is a 'lossless' tool, which means it optimizes the images without changing their look or visual quality.

You can enter multiple image URL addresses from your site, and Smush. it will report how many bytes would be saved by optimizing the images. Handily, it will then provide a downloadable zip file with the minimized image files.

You can also upload images to compress, which can then be downloaded as a zip archive.

Optimizilla
Website: http://optimizilla.com

Optimizilla allows you to upload up to 20 files in JPEG and PNG formats. You can then use the slider to control the compression level and download the results. Optimizilla uses a smart combination of the best optimization and lossy compression algorithms to shrink an image file to the minimum possible size while keeping the required level of quality.

CompressNow
Website: http://compressnow.com

A nice and easy tool to use—just choose your percentage of compression level, upload your image and view the result. Supported file types are GIF, JPG, JPEG and PNG.

Case Study—Creating a Prototype in Unity

I recently created a Prototype within Unity for a game called Vektor Wars. I have included the early development diaries here, as it covers working on a project in Unity from conception, and highlights some great Asset Store assets.

Development Diary—Part One

Vektor Wars is a first-person combat game. Players compete for the global highest scores in a battle of combat skills between the player and the unstoppable enemy forces. Featuring a modern take on vector style graphics, Vektor Wars is a classic arcade shooter where the only things that matter are your game skills and the high score!

With graphics to make your eyes sing and a powerful John Carpenter–influenced soundtrack, this in an epic first-person combat experience!

Vektor Wars is primarily a solo project of mine—one that I have wanted to do for a very long time.

Influences

I used to love the old '80s-style computer wireframe sequences and visual styling from movies like *Escape from New York, Terminator, Tron*—bright, super-saturated computer wireframe imagery. Also, the classic early vector 3D games like Elite, Starglider, Mercenary and

Figure 1.1 Vektor Wars logo

Battlezone—I spent many happy hours playing those games, and I don't think I've ever topped that feeling of immersion from exploring those early 3D worlds.

So, although I had wanted to do a game like this for a long time, I never really had the tech or resources to do it; we were doing other things and the opportunity never really arose.

Enter Unity and a little bit of experimentation, and all of a sudden the game I always wanted to make started to become a reality.

While it is still relatively early on in development, a lot of the basics are in place.

Visuals

Glowing neon wireframes galore! But I didn't want to just stick to wireframes, so I have textured all of the buildings too—with heavily stylized windows, signs, lights, adverts and so on. The vectors were

Figure 1.2 Vecktor Wars screenshot

created by importing the 3D meshes, then effectively joining the dots (vertices) in the models. I then had to remove all the tripled lines to give the impression of n-sided wireframes. The lines themselves are rendered with a texture with a white line in the middle and graduated alpha edges—so it blends out to transparency and gives a nice glowing effect.

I used an Asset Store plugin to handle the vectors, called Vectrosity:

▶ https://www.assetstore.unity3d.com/en/#!/content/82

It was super easy to set up and implement. I just followed the help guides, and within an hour or so I had glowing vectors!

Another thing I am really pleased with are the neon sign animations—they work a treat and really enhance the atmosphere and feeling of life. These are simply texture sheets, with an adapted version of this script:

▶ http://wiki.unity3d.com/index.php/Animating_Tiled_texture

Code

Initially I concentrated on getting the 3D world and visual effects in place, which was fairly quick to do. Gameplay code is proving to be great fun to do, and is shaping up really well, thanks again to the Asset Store. So, what have I used?

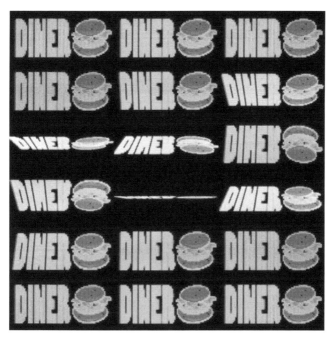

Figure 1.3 Neon signs—texture animation sheet

Game Control

The first-person interface, control and combat are handled by this most excellent Unity package Ultimate FPS. Basically, it does all of the FPS basics REALLY well, saving months of work, and it costs—drum roll—$15! Yep only 15 dollars to save months of work and thousands in coding costs.

You can find the UFPS plugin here:
https://www.assetstore.unity3d.com/en/#!/content/2943

AI and Pathfinding

So with that in place things are rolling along nicely, a rock solid control and combat system—a system like that deserves some rather good AI. Step-up Aron Granburg and his fantastic A* Pathfinding Project. After half a day, I had an enemy who would follow you anywhere on the map—then gun you down like a dog! He was relentless and unstoppable and had one purpose in (artificial) life: to kill you!

I sat there with a big grin on my face being chased around by this angry capsule (the default Unity capsule object). Now things were taking shape!

Since then I have refined the AI, adding in some modifiers to the path following, and thanks to Steve (Super Icon's resident coder) a nice simple AI attack script was added and a few other bits and pieces. Rock solid AI, nice.

Find out more about A* here:
http://arongranberg.com/astar/

Enemies

I'm currently modelling a batch of different enemies (spot the influences!), and we have both raycast enemy shooting (i.e. instant hit from something like a machine gun) and projectiles with nice glowing trails. Over the next few days I'll be focusing on creating a unique AI for each enemy—so they attack differently, have weapons with different power and ranges, and all the other good stuff!

I have put together a map of the first world with key landmarks—the City of New Hope (see Figure 1.5).

In recent weeks, I have made some really good progress and understand Unity a lot more now too. So far I'm loving it, in particular the Asset Store, which is an amazing resource.

So a quick recap on Vektor Wars: it is a retro vector GFX first-person shooter. Visually, it is an homage to the whole '80s sci-fi/wireframe

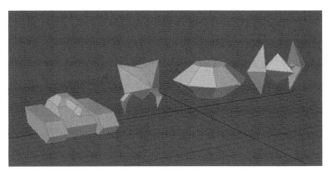

Figure 1.4 First Vektor Wars enemies

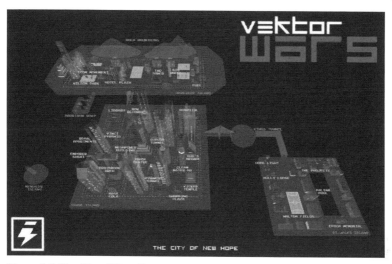

Figure 1.5 The City of New Hope

look with gameplay influenced by a love of classic shooters such as Battlezone, Bezerk and Encounter.

Development Diary—Part Two

Since part one, a lot of stuff has been added—player weapons, pick-up system, the first batch of enemies, sound effects, particle effects and other eye-candy along with a more cohesive design and plan for the different game modes and special collectibles.

So, what's new . . .?

Player Weapons

We've added the first pass of the player weapons—I think you could call this the Doom weapon edition as we have added the basic, familiar sounding weapons:

- ▶ Pistol
- ▶ Mini-gun
- ▶ Super shotgun
- ▶ Plasma gun
- ▶ Rockets
- ▶ Laser blaster
- ▶ BFG (and its green!)

This is a nice core set of weapons to get started with. I will also be adding a few more, which I shall have more details on in the next update.

I tried various experiments with different graphic styles for the on-screen guns, but couldn't really get anything that looked right—so in the end I ditched the on-screen weapons and went for a different HUD style approach. The different weapons each have their own unique HUD graphics and cursors, with muzzle flash animations, and the HUDs move and bob as you move and look around. I like it—it feels very '80s VR and a bit Iron Man–ish.

Score Flash

As scoring will be the main focus of the game, I wanted to have a nice visual system for presenting score updates and other game messages. I found a plugin called Score Flash, which does just the job—so now all game messages go through this with the text scaling up and fading out nicely. You can also add it to the enemies, so it gets drawn in 3D space, for example, when you destroy an enemy.

You can find Score Flash here:
https://www.assetstore.unity3d.com/en/#!/content/4476

Enemies So Far

For the first world I have added seven different enemies, which range from a lightweight grunt-type enemy through to a master robot-style enemy.

Figure 1.6 HUD overlays

Figure 1.7 Vektor Wars trading cards

I've put together a few trading cards above to show the enemy designs and stats so far.

Explosion Effects

I wanted to make the explosions fit in with the vector style, so geometric shapes with lots of glow but not at all realistic looking. Unity particles are very flexible, so with a bit of practice it was easy to make up an explosion with a few different components (a central core that expands, light beams expanding out and Defender-style square particle showers).

I also plugged Score Flash in here so that when you destroy the enemy the score displays too—and takes into account the current score multiplier. Nice and arcadey!

These Asset Store particle effects came in handy too:
8-bit inspired particles—https://www.assetstore.unity3d.com/en/#!/content/10462
Vectormania!—https://www.assetstore.unity3d.com/en/#!/content/2663

Enemy AI

Plenty more tinkering has been going on here (with Steve's coding help), and it is getting better and better. I have spent a lot of time tweaking

Figure 1.8 Retro explosion goodness

speed, aim, damage and other core values to get the basic feeling right. I encountered one issue with the enemies falling in the water—took ages to suss this out. Basically they were going too close to the edge of the ground and then dropping off into the water, and because they weren't allowed to be there they got horribly confused.

In the end it was a super simple fix—in A* there is an Erosion iterations setting. I upped this to one and that brought the grid in away from the edges and no more falling enemies!

Retro Computer System

Since day one, I have wanted to get a retro-style computer interface in there—similar in function to those menus you had when logging onto computer consoles in games like Paradroid and Alien Breed. Visually/design-wise I wanted a real retro feel for this, similar to the computer displays you used to see in '80s sci-fi movies and TV shows.

Initially we are going to have two game modes—an arcade mode and a story mode; and it is the story mode I had in mind with the computer system stuff. Your PDA will receive messages from home that will start to tell a story about you, your background and about what is happening with the robot invasion.

So, I got cracking with a GUI tool and started laying out a few screens and adding text via an external text file (so it is easy to edit and ready for if we localise the languages). I also wanted to get a scan lines effect, which was nice and easily achieved by overlaying an alpha lines texture onto the camera. One slight bummer is that our budget at the moment doesn't stretch to Unity Pro licences. I'd have loved to experiment with some chromatic aberration/analogue TV type full-screen effects.

The plugin I used was called NGUI, and it is the most popular Unity GUI system around.
https://www.assetstore.unity3d.com/en/#!/content/2413

I used fonts that matched closely to those used in the reference images I collected, and I must admit I have based the player's PDA readouts quite heavily on the old C64 boot screen. It took me ages to find a good sound effect that didn't grate on the ears to accompany the tele-type text animation.

The dafont site was very useful here:
http://www.dafont.com/

In addition to your PDA interface, there will be computer consoles in the levels that you can log onto. These will all look different—with black and red, green screen monitor and other colour schemes, possibly more influences from other '80s computers like Commodore Pet, ZX Spectrum etc.

Transition Effects

With every game I've ever worked on we've stuck with either a fade to black, or if we were feeling fancy, a whiteout. Never really had the time or know-how to do a decent system of video-style fades and transitions. Once again the Asset Store was on hand, and we found a nice script called 'Easy Masking Transition' that uses Luma Matte textures to fade to black (or any other colour). Very clever stuff it is too—basically the matte textures are just greyscale images and these determine how the fade happens. The lighter and darker areas fade in at different rates—so it appears to animate and you can do all sorts of funky transitions.

Easy Masking Transition can be found here:
https://www.assetstore.unity3d.com/en/#!/content/8734

City Map Tweaks

I tweaked a few bits and pieces in the city—added detail on the rooftops, added a few more buildings and monuments. I also changed the bridges around and made them wider so the enemy AI can cross them easier.

There are also ladders in the water now, and we have started adding in the special PowerCubes you need to explore and collect. We really want to encourage plenty of exploration. I have to add a glider/jetpack in there!

The pickups system is all done now for weapons, ammo, multiplier tokens, power-ups and so on. I'd say world one is just about ready to go now . . .

Enemy Waves

Oh—nearly forgot—enemy waves. Again another Asset Store job here: Killer Waves (now renamed to Core GameKit), which has given us a robust system to add enemy waves and levels easily. I am currently playing with the first-level waves and I'm getting something solid now. This was the point it started to feel like a game, which was very exciting, and a little daunting.

Core GameKit can be found here:
https://www.assetstore.unity3d.com/en/#!/content/6640

Sound Effects

I donned my headphones again and got stuck into the sound effects. I have some really nice sounds now for the weapons—good meaty sounds that really pack a punch.

Enemy sounds are also taking shape—I have been experimenting with Bezerk-style robot speech effects. I used the speech synth in FL Studio (v11) and ran the results through a couple of effects, including the brilliant FL Vocodex. They sound good and threatening now—but I do need to make a few of them a little clearer so you can understand what is being shouted at you.

FL Studio is a good choice for music and sound effects, and is one of the lower cost DAWs (Digital Audio Workstations):
http://www.image-line.com/flstudio/

And last, spot effects—using a few C64 style SID sounds—I'm just deciding if they fit at the moment.

What's Next?

I am planning a funded Alpha or Early Access. This seems a good approach because it allows me to really get chatting with the community and get feedback as I progress. I love the idea of user input through the later design stages; it seems to me that is what the spirit of indie development is really about.

I am still thinking over the plans, but one thing is for sure—the lead SKUs will be the computer formats (PC and Mac), so I am trying to brush up on my knowledge of releasing indie games on computer.

Developing Our First Unity Game

At Super Icon, our first live project using Unity was a brick-breaker called 'Brick Break Blitz'.

This was a really fun project to work on, and actually the first time I had ever really programmed (I learnt the basics of C# for the project). My coding was shaky though, so Steve was on-hand to help and handle the trickier bits.

The Unity wiki was also very helpful, with lots of code examples and advice:
http://wiki.unity3d.com/index.php/Main_Page

The Answers section on the Unity community site is another brilliant place to get coding advice:
http://answers.unity3d.com

To get things up and running as swiftly as possible, I used one of the Asset Store project templates: the Advanced Breakout Kit (https://www.assetstore.unity3d.com/en/#!/content/5763). It was a good starting point, although truth be told, we ended up re-writing most of it.

Once the kit was installed, my next task was to prepare the graphics. I used Lightwave 3D to create all of the meshes, with the exception of those I purchased from the Asset Store (which I'll cover in a moment). The models I created included the bricks, ball, paddle, walls, backgrounds and enemies.

In order to get the meshes into Unity, I had to export from Lightwave in FBX format. FBXs are a little tricky as they are supported via a plugin, so not as reliable as native Lightwave objects (LWOs). That said, it didn't really cause any issues.

Unity Shaders

The next stage was to tweak the shaders used for rendering the meshes. I used a combination of the Unity default mobile-friendly normal mapping shader and the following shader add-ons, again from the Asset Store:

Gem Shader—https://www.assetstore.unity3d.com/en/#!/content/3
This is a free shader created by Unity, which renders gem-like surfaces—and they look great.

Metal Cubicmap volume 1—https://www.assetstore.unity3d.com/en/#!/content/3949
Cubicmap is used slightly differently, in that I used the mobile-friendly simple reflection map surface, and applied one of these cubic map textures. The results were brilliant—perfect looking metal, yet optimised for mobiles. I used this for the metallic balls, paddle, bricks and metal walls.

Creating the Levels

Then came the tricky bit: creating the levels. The Breakout Kit only included one level, and that was populated by hand (i.e. positioning the meshes via the Unity scene editor). Not an ideal solution, to say the least!

After a little head scratching, I decided the best approach was to try a tile painting system. These are typically used for games like platformers, where you position the platform tiles around, but of course they lend themselves well to a block-based breakout type game.

I settled on the Rotorz Tile System in the end, and it worked like a charm. Each of the game bricks were converted to Rotorz brushes, set within a grid size of 16 blocks wide by 12 blocks high. I could then easily paint with the brick brushes for each level, which allowed me to populate levels quickly and easily.

Rotorz can be found here:
https://www.assetstore.unity3d.com/en/#!/content/3344

Special Effects

Next up were effects and particles. Again, I used Score Flash for the in-game messages, and the 8-bit style particles for explosions and impacts. I also created a few particle effects of my own—once you get started with Unity particles, it is fairly easy to get some good stuff going. Work from example particle systems, study how they are setup, and then start trying to create your own.

Another plugin that came in very useful was Particle Scaler, which allowed me to tweak the overall sizes of the particle effects with a single scale setting, rather than having to modify each element of the particle effect individually. You can find Particle Scaler here:
https://www.assetstore.unity3d.com/en/#!/content/4400

One more plugin that I can't recommend highly enough is the Advance PlayerPrefs Window. The Unity PlayerPrefs are where you store things like save data, player progress, options settings and so on. The PlayerPrefs window allows you to view all of these at once, watch real-time updates and edit/delete prefs as you wish. You NEED this plugin!
https://www.assetstore.unity3d.com/en/#!/content/7070

I included four different 'themes' within the game, an 'Arkanoid' style metallic theme, an underwater theme, a space theme and a cloudy sky theme. Again, the Asset Store came in useful here, in particular the Unluck Software particle sets, such as Toon Clouds:
https://www.assetstore.unity3d.com/en/#!/content/8225

I also needed a few extra meshes for 'enemies'—basically obstacles that float around and impede the ball movement. So I added crystals with the gem shader and asteroids (https://www.assetstore.unity3d.com/en/#!/content/7315), rubber duckies, treasure chests (https://www.assetstore.unity3d.com/en/#!/content/9057) and more.

And there we have it—lots of testing and tweaking later, one Unity game ready to go out into the wild!

Insider Indie Q&A

1. *What is the name of your studio?*

   Disco Pixel

   # Disco Pixel

   © 2007 Disco Pixel

2. *What year was your studio founded and what are the names of the founders?*

   2007 by Trevor Stricker and Noah Heller. (We both went on hiatus ~2008: Trevor to start Quickhit Football, Noah to be the product director of Call of Duty. Trevor came back in 2012.)

3. *What are the studio's key game titles?*

   Jungle Rumble: Freedom, Happiness and Bananas

4. *Do you have your own in-house engine or use a third party system? If third party, which one do you use?*

   Unity

5. *Which platforms do you release on now / plan to release on?*

   We're out on iOS, coming to Android and PS Vita

6. *Which is your most successful platform so far?*

   iPad. Interestingly, our biggest country is Japan.

7. *What are the development tools you use most (i.e. 2D, 3D software, audio tools etc.)?*

   Luigi Guatieri, our artist, uses Photoshop and Illustrator.

   Richard Gould, our musician, uses Bang Box. Jungle Rumble has a dynamic soundtrack that is composited from samples at runtime. Bang Box is our sequencer. We're releasing it later as a free app.

8. *What advice would you give to a new studio?*

   Ask yourself, what makes you want to start a studio? This is a high mortality business. And loving to play video games doesn't mean you will be good at making them. I mean, I love R. Kelly but I'll spare you my rendition of 'I Believe I Can Fly'. If you want to make games and have people play them, in the age of Unity and digital distribution and the internet you can do that on the side with a 'real' job—and possibly be happier. Don't think you have to dive into being a full-time indie. Releasing some hobby projects is a valid way to see if you can really do this long term. Working at a larger studio is another way to learn about making games while having a paycheck.

Go into this with your eyes open. It will take longer to make your game than you think, and it will probably have less revenue.

9. *What marketing resources do you use?*

I love going to cons and showing Jungle Rumble to gamers. Connecting with people who love games. It's the best.

I have an email list that I send out news and promo codes for friends' games on. You can sign up at our website.

10. *What are your favourite indie games sites?*

If "indie" is a hard to define term for games, then it's even harder to use for websites. I love the attitude and breadth of Indie Statik. Gamasutra is great, but not really game news. Polygon has some great in-depth coverage.

11. *Any mistakes/hiccups you have made so far, something you would advise a new studio to avoid?*

I think we rushed Jungle Rumble out the door. It was ready. But we could have done much more work raising awareness before shipping.

CHAPTER **2**
Self-Publishing

The games industry has changed so much over recent years. The shift from publisher-funded publishing to developer self-publishing has seen so many exciting and wonderful opportunities open up for developers. Who would have thought a few years ago that this would ever happen? At the time developers were firmly in the control of publishers and the platform holders, getting a game to market could often be a very difficult process. I'll illustrate this with an example of how it used to be . . .

In 2005, my studio signed a deal with a small US publisher to publish two of our games in North America on PS2 and PSP. The deal was negotiated by an agency on our behalf and was worth $450,000 for us. This was huge—the games were complete, already released in PAL territories and ready to go into SCEA QA.

And then, the kick in the teeth . . . Sony of America refused concept approval, and the deal was dead—no negotiation—finished. Overnight we lost a $450,000 deal, which for a small studio like ours would have drastically improved our position and helped us to invest more money into future development. And these were games already released in the PAL region with some fairly good reviews!

This hit me really hard; it took a long time for me to get over the setback and the unfairness of it all. At the time, it was very difficult to try to forget and to focus on new developments, especially as our cash flow projections had been destroyed in one step. We had the deal signed, and while they weren't stellar games, there were hundreds of titles out there with much lower review scores on PSP and PS2. These were solid games; the difference was that we were a small UK indie studio, SCEA didn't know us and our publisher wasn't one of the bigger publishers. Effectively, we were beaten before we even submitted; we just didn't know it at the time. For a long time I didn't even want to think about working with Sony again!

Fast forward eight years, and Sony are now the most indie-friendly of all the platform holders, actively seeking and funding indie content. They have removed the old concept approval process, they are responsive and great to work with and they even give free development kits to indies! What a difference, and what a fantastic progression that represents for independent developers all over the world.

Self-publishing offers indie studios complete freedom over what they do, the games they make and the platforms they release on. There is now a massive community of like-minded fellow indies out there, sharing experiences and information, passing on help and advice. Never be afraid to speak to other developers to ask advice; many will help and it is my belief that if we as developers share our knowledge, it benefits us all.

It really is a fantastic time to be an indie games developer right now!

Base Game Projects

Aim to build up a number of 'base' game projects and routines to use as the foundation for new titles. This can save a lot of time and allow you to prototype quickly—thus allowing you to focus on the gameplay and content rather than trying to reinvent the wheel each time you develop a new title.

By way of an example, at Super Icon we currently have several types of base projects in the bag, and we add to these continually. At the time of writing we have the following projects ready to go as we need: Air

Hockey, Ball Rolling/Balance (Monkey Ball/Marble Madness style), Board Games (such as Battleships, Connect 4, Hangman, Draughts), Bowling, Breakout/Arkanoid, Crazy Golf, Darts, FPS, Motor Racing (with in-game track creation functionality), Pool and Snooker and a very robust 2D platform game system. I know that I can reuse any of those base projects to hit the ground running on a new game, and potentially save many man months of work. This is particularly useful if you are operating in the work-for-hire field; you can pitch for certain projects knowing that you could be up and running quicker with a solid first playable in a relatively short time-frame.

This then leaves the decision of which platform(s) to target, so let's take a look at the various platforms available right now. It is a big and ever-growing list, as there really are a wealth of systems and publishing options out there.

What I would say, particularly if you are a smaller studio, is to try to focus on one key launch system and put all of your efforts into that. Don't try to develop multiple SKUs at once, as it can be rather overwhelming to develop, balance and test on multiple devices concurrently. If you do plan to release on other systems later, make sure you include details of that in your marketing, so that you can start building up interest for all platforms early on in development.

Publishing on PC

The PC games market has seen something of a renaissance over the last few years, with game sales approaching those in the early '90s PC heyday. Many of the well-known indie success stories, games such as Minecraft, Thomas Was Alone, Hotline Miami and The Stanley Parable, launched on PC. These are games that made their creators millionaires, and earned them celebrity status within the games industry.

It is really exciting to see the fortunes of PC gaming improving, as it offers indie developers a great low-cost entry point to game development, without any of the hassles involved with creating games for consoles or the technical restrictions of mobile platforms.

On the flip side, it can be difficult to make money given the massive number of indie PC titles out there. Compared to a console game, a

PC-only title usually requires far more of a PR and marketing push before it starts selling decent numbers.

So, without further ado, let's take a look at the various aspects of PC game publishing.

Playable Free Alpha Demo

A good approach to try to build a pre-release audience is to release a free Alpha demo on sites such as Kongregate.com and indiedb.com.

This demo build is a limited version, with perhaps an hour or so of gameplay and a handful of near final quality levels. You must make sure that you detail in full what the release version will offer, and crucially, a link to where players can pre-order the final game. Be specific and avoid the situation where players judge an Alpha demo as final quality; it can make sense to include a line in your release notes explicitly stating that the Alpha demo isn't a fully polished, final quality version—it is a work-in-progress.

Consider also including a mailing list sign-up form to gather player contact details, so that you can notify them of the game's progress, new features and release schedule.

Early Access Release

This is a fairly recent development. Early Access is a funding model by which consumers can pay for a game in the early stages of development and obtain access to playable but unfinished versions of the game, while the developer is able to use those funds to continue work on the game. One of the biggest players in Early Access development is Valve, and the Steam platform, and this is the Steam definition of Early Access:

"Get immediate access to games that are being developed with the community's involvement. These are games that evolve as you play them, as you give feedback, and as the developers update and add content.

We like to think of games and game development as services that grow and evolve with the involvement of customers and the community. There have been a number of prominent titles that have embraced this model of development recently and found a lot of value in the process. We like to support and encourage developers who want to ship early, involve customers, and build lasting relationships that help everyone make better games. This is the way games should be made."

From a developer perspective, Early Access is an ideal way to help fund indie development. I really like the idea of the community getting involved with the development, helping to shape the game. You can also add extra incentives, such as an additional free copy for a friend. Don't do this too early though as you need to make sure the initial Early Access build gives a good idea of the release game and is fun to play.

Installers

When self-publishing on PC, you may well need to create an installer. The last time I self-published a PC title I researched a number of different solutions including Nullsoft Scriptable Install System and Astrum Install Wizard. I chose Astrum at the time as it was the easiest and quickest to implement, and there were a few decent interface skins available. Unfortunately Astrum is now out of date and obsolete.

After researching a whole load of indie PC games, my conclusion is that there are two popular choices:

NSIS (Nullsoft Scriptable Install System)
Website: http://nsis.sourceforge.net/Main_Page

A professional open source system to create Windows installers. It is designed to be as small and flexible as possible and is therefore very suitable for internet distribution.

Inno Setup
Website: http://www.jrsoftware.org/isinfo.php

Inno Setup is a free installer for Windows programs. First introduced in 1997, Inno Setup today rivals and even surpasses many commercial installers in feature set and stability.

I decided to go with Inno, and it is great. A breeze to set up, very reliable and it gets the job done with minimal hassle.

DRM

Next up is the thorny issue of DRM. At the most basic level, Digital Rights Management (DRM) technologies are used to curb piracy by restricting users' ability to copy software, though it can also be used to create new business models, like subscriptions.

DRM was very widely used in games, but opinions are changing and now most indies no longer bother with DRM. That said, it can still have its uses providing you do it in such a way that won't alienate paying customers. There are three approaches you can take to DRM:

DRM Free

Very much the consumer choice and favoured by a lot of indie developers. Very easy to implement as you don't actually have to do anything, but certainly the most open to piracy.

Separate Demo and Full Version

Completely separate builds with the demo freely available to download, often with features and content cut so it can't be hacked to run the full version. The full version is then available to download from a password-protected site once purchased, with the download details emailed to the customer. I initially decided this was too much hassle and time intensive, having to maintain two separate builds, but I am warming to this approach now.

Commercial DRM Solutions

Purchase a package and with a bit of setting up you can control licensing and activation and the terms of the trial (i.e. 60 minutes' free play, x number of free plays, x days and so on). I have used this method in the past as it was the most convenient solution for managing the licensing for multiple titles.

You can also develop your own soft-touch DRM, basically an email registration and key delivery system.

I can't say I would recommend commercial DRM now, as most indie titles these days are DRM free and consumers tend to react badly to DRM, unless it is part of a service such as Steam.

For completeness sake, I have included a few commercial solutions below:

ExeShield
Website: http://www.exeshield.com

With ExeShield it's easy to turn your applications into 'try before you buy' software with very little effort, and maximum protection against piracy, backdating, reverse engineering or any kind of tampering.

Win License
Website: http://www.oreans.com/winlicense.php

WinLicense combines the same protection-level as Themida with the power of advanced licence control, offering the most powerful and flexible technology that allows developers to securely distribute trial and registered versions of their applications.

Selling a PC Game

The first option, and one that can be run alongside other sales activities, is to sell directly via your own website. What you do need to decide on is an e-commerce partner—the most popular choices for indies are BMT Micro, FastSpring and PayPal. Or you can use a widget like the Humble Widget.

Look for a low royalty rate (no more than 10%) and solid customer service. Several of the e-commerce providers will also work with you to set up a customized, secure store page to match the look of your company website.

On the subject of websites, make sure you register a proper domain name with a good, reliable webhost. There is nothing worse than hosting on a site that fails as soon as you get a few people connecting at once. Your site MUST be rock solid as it is from here they will purchase your game!

The most popular e-commerce systems for indie developers right now are:

Humble Store Widget
Website: https://www.humblebundle.com/forms

Simply put, the Humble Widget is brilliant. We used this for our recent PC/Mac game release, Life of Pixel, and it made the sales process nice and easy.

Humble collect the payments and transfer the revenue to you directly each month. Customers have the option to pay via PayPal and Amazon Payments. Humble also host the builds and/or fulfil third-party key purchases (e.g. Steam keys). Builds are delivered to your customers using the Humble Bundle digital distribution platform.

Humble also provide customer support for basic questions concerning purchasing or downloading content. Any subtle questions concerning the actual game will be forwarded to you directly.

There is also an easy to use admin dashboard, where you can monitor sales, generate promotion/review codes as and when you need and grant refunds to customers. You also have a full list of all the people who have purchased your game, including their email addresses.

Revenue splits—after deductions for payment processor fees (typically around 5%), the net revenue is split 95% to the developer, and 5% to Humble Bundle. VAT is deducted where applicable.

BMT Micro
Website: http://www.bmtmicro.com

BMT Micro has been providing turnkey e-commerce solutions since 1992. If you require a reliable, cost-effective payment processing service that is flexible enough to meet your needs now and well into the future, look no further.

Fee: 9.5% (Minimum fee of $1.25)
Payment options: Credit card, PayPal, Google Checkout, Amazon Payments, check, instant bank transfer, wire transfer, phone/fax

FastSpring
Website: http://www.fastspring.com

FastSpring offers a highly customizable, flexible e-commerce solution focused on adding value and increasing revenue for clients, while providing the best customer service in the industry.

Fee: 8.9% (Minimum fee of $0.75)
Payment options: Credit card, PayPal

PayPal
Website: https://www.paypal.com/

Everything you need to get paid, faster. Accept payments securely on your website, on eBay, by email and from mobiles. One solution handles it all.

One-stop-shop payment provider, a PayPal business account is all you need. No set-up fees, no monthly fees, and no cancellation fees.

Fee: 2.9% + $0.30 per item
Payment options: Credit card, PayPal
Notes: You will be charged 3.9% + $0.30 for payments outside of the US. You also need to handle hosting the games yourself and the sales taxes.

Direct Sales

Direct sales earn you around 90% of each sale, so if you get them right they can be very lucrative indeed. Cliff Harris of Positech Games is something of a success story with direct sales of his games, and he has this to say on the subject: "Direct sales grow over time. It took me maybe five years before I could live from my direct sales, and was able to quit my job. Are you prepared to make an investment now that will pay off in the long run? Are you not even prepared to put an hour or two a week into developing the direct sales part of your business? If the answer is no, make sure you have a good business case for that. Not an emotional one. Direct sales are an insurance policy."

If you are selling directly from your website MAKE SURE your website hosting package includes plenty of bandwidth and won't fail if too many visitors connect to your site at once. At Super Icon, we were using a shared server on DreamHost. This proved to be a disaster when we hosted a couple of our own game demos a few years ago.

As soon as more than a few visitors tried to access the site and download, the site went down. The reason for this was that the shared server policy will disable your site if there is too much traffic. The justification being that they have to stop individual sites taking too much of the bandwidth for the server, and thus leaving the other hosted sites without enough bandwidth. Every time our site got busy, the same thing would happen, so not at all suitable for direct sales. Use online tools to measure load speeds. Unless you have a killer hosting plan, it is unlikely your site would be able to handle multiple downloads of large files without grinding to a halt, or worse, failing completely.

Post a Demo on Kongregate

A good strategy to follow with direct sales is to release a demo on Kongregate (http://developers.kongregate.com) to help boost traffic to your site. Kong has a huge audience, so potentially you can drive extra direct sales by releasing a game demo on there.

Many indie developers have recommended this approach to boost direct sales, and there are a few other perks too:

▶ You can earn up to 50% of the ad revenue generated on your game's page. Note: there are certain restrictions in place that you must follow to increase revenue share up from the default 25%

▶ With kreds, Kong's virtual currency, developers can make much more by charging for items and content in-game.

▶ Kongregate has unique opportunities to promote your game to the millions of consumers who shop at GameStop, the world's largest video games retailer.

The one (potentially major) downside is that your game has to run in a browser to host on Kong.

Bundles

Right now a large section of the PC gaming audience currently appear to have two tactics when it comes to buying new PC games:

"I'll buy it when it's on Steam."

Or

"I'll buy it when it's in a bundle."

I'll cover Steam later in this chapter, but Bundles can be very worthwhile indeed; often shifting some amazing numbers, particularly the big-hitters such as the 'Humble Bundle'.

The Long-Tail

Bundles are a good way to help maintain the long-tail period of your game's lifespan, in addition to other sales and discount promotions.

There are several marketing-speak definitions of long-tail on the internet, but essentially it is the time after the release-period sales have died down, where online retailers can make more money than their bricks and mortar counterparts because there is virtually unlimited 'shelf space' to offer products.

Every indie developer should try to maximize their profits over time and these types of promotions can really give your decreasing long-tail sales a boost.

Here are a few of the most popular Bundle promotion sites:

Humble Bundle
Website: https://www.humblebundle.com/

Pay what you want—name your price and increase your contribution to get even more.

Access on Steam—pay $1 or more for access to these games on Steam.

Support charity—choose exactly how your purchase is divided between the developers, charity or even the Humble tip jar.

Indie Royale
Website: http://www.indieroyale.com/

Indie Royale is an indie game bundle website that offers up multiple top-quality indie titles every two weeks for you to purchase at seriously silly prices. All you need to do is pay the price stated—or pay more—and the games currently featured will be yours to keep forever.

The point of Indie Royale is to put the spotlight on those indie titles that provide fantastic experiences, but may well have been passed over by a good portion of the mainstream gaming public. If you purchase an Indie Royale bundle, you can be safe in the knowledge that you're not only getting multiple brilliant indie games—you're also supporting worthwhile developers.

Bundle Stars
Website: http://www.bundlestars.com/

Get awesome game bundles
Redeem on Steam
Make colossal savings

Publishing on Game Portals

If you are publishing a PC or Mac game, it is a good idea to release your game on several of the game portal sites. You will usually be looking at a 70/30 revenue split, and you shouldn't encounter any exclusivity issues. Be aware though that inclusion on some of the portals won't really boost sales by much. From personal experience and reports from other developers, sales on sites such as Amazon, Desura, Gamers Gate, Impulse can be very low indeed. On the upside though, any sales are good and it all helps to boost your studio coffers.

The portal of choice is most definitely Steam. In every indie sales report I've seen, Steam sales eclipse all other portals by a large margin, often selling several times more than on other portal sites.

Key Portals

These are the portals that are reported to give the highest sales numbers after Steam.

GOG
Website: http://www.gog.com/

Revenue split: 70% (developer) / 30% (GOG)
Contact details: Contact them via their website here—http://www.gog.com/indie
Monetisation: Outright sale

I have read several blog posts from indie developers confirming that GOG is the second choice behind Steam in terms of volume of sales. I am sure this does vary from game to game, and Humble Bundle sales often eclipse everything in terms of numbers. Nonetheless, the stats are impressive, so GOG is definitely one to try.

Games must be DRM free to release on GOG.

Humble Store
Website: https://www.humblebundle.com/store

Revenue split: 75% (developer) / 10% (charity) / 15% (Humble Bundle)
Contact details: Contact them via their website form here: https://www.
humblebundle.com/forms
Monetisation: Outright sale

The Humble Store is a good place to be, especially if you can get
included within a Humble Bundle, which sell in huge numbers
(although the revenue per sale for each game in the bundle is relatively
low). Games must be DRM-free.

Gamers Gate
Website: http://www.gamersgate.co.uk/

Revenue split: 70% (developer) / 30% (Gamers Gate)
Contact details: Email them at publisher@gamersgate.com with details
of your games
Monetisation: Outright sale, free to play and DLC

There is a specific indie sales section on Gamers Gate called 'Indiefort',
so they take their indie games seriously. Again, mixed reports on sales
numbers, but certainly Gamers Gate offers one of the better portal
solutions.

Amazon US
Website: https://developer.amazon.com/public/solutions/platforms/
mac-pc

Revenue split: 70% (developer) / 30% (Amazon)
Contact details: Sign up for a developer account, and then submit
your game
Monetisation: Outright sale

Amazon's Digital Software store offers you a distribution channel to
promote and sell your software and subscriptions to millions of Amazon
customers. Includes the Indie Games Store, which is a dedicated
storefront designed to specifically help indie game developers with

promoting their PC, Mac and browser-based games while helping gamers discover a large and growing selection of innovative indie games.

Green Man Gaming
Website: http://www.greenmangaming.com

Revenue split: 70% (developer) / 30% (Green Man)
Contact details: Email them at nick.ashley@greenmangaming.com with details of your games
Monetisation: Outright sale

Green Man Gaming is another portal with a prominent indie specific section. As yet I haven't seen much data for indie sales numbers.

Desura
Website: http://www.desura.com/

Revenue split: 70% (developer) / 30% (Desura)
Contact details: Submit via their website here: http://www.desura.com/ development, or create a game profile on IndieDB/ModDB and publish the game
Monetisation: Outright sale, free to play, DLC and Alpha funding

Desura is a nice platform in many ways, and very developer friendly. Unfortunately, sales numbers can be poor, so it is hard to say just how valuable Desura is as a service. Most indies do tend to release on Desura, but all the reports I've seen so far have shown fairly low numbers.

Other Portals to Consider

Big Fish Games
Website: http://www.bigfishgames.com/
Revenue split: Negotiable; usually on the low side for the developer
Contact details: Email them at freetoplaysubmissions@bigfishgames. com with a free to play title, or premiumsubmissions@bigfishgames. com with a premium title
Monetisation: Outright sale and free to play

GameFly
Website: http://digital.gamefly.co.uk

Revenue split: Negotiable
Contact details: Contact them via their website here: http://www.
gamefly.co.uk/support/gameflydigital/contact/#.Um6xkZGpojI
Monetisation: Outright sale and DLC

GameHouse
Website: http://www.gamehouse.com/

Revenue split: Negotiable
Contact details: Contact them via their website here: http://partners.
gamehouse.com
Monetisation: Outright sale and DLC

GameStop/Impulse
Website: http://www.impulsedriven.com/publisher/independent

Revenue split: 70% (developer) / 30% (Impulse)
Contact details: Contact them via their website here: https://developer.
impulsedriven.com
Monetisation: Outright sale and DLC

GamesPlanet
Website: http://gamesplanet.com

Revenue split: Unknown
Contact details: Contact them via email: business@metaboli.co.uk
Monetisation: Outright sale and DLC. They also run a crowdfunding
site: http://www.lab.gamesplanet.com

GameTree Mac
Website: https://gametreemac.com/

Revenue split: Unknown
Contact details: Contact them via their website here: https://
gametreemac.com/contact-us/
Monetisation: Outright sale

Get Games
Website: http://www.getgamesgo.com/

Revenue split: 70% (developer) / 30% (GetGames)
Contact details: Contact them via their website here: http://www.
getgamesgo.com/support
Monetisation: Outright sale and DLC

IndieCity
Website: http://store.indiecity.com/

Revenue split: 75% (developer) / 25% (IndieCity) or 85% (developer) /
15% (IndieCity) if you incorporate their ICELib SDK in your game
Contact details: Register and add your game(s) to the site
Monetisation: Outright sale

Mac Game Store
Website: http://www.macgamestore.com/

Revenue split: Unknown
Contact details: Contact them via their website here: https://www.
macgamestore.com/information/Publishers/
Monetisation: Outright sale and DLC

Wild Tangent
Website: http://www.wildtangent.com/

Revenue split: Unknown
Contact details: Contact them via their website here: http://www.
wildtangent.com/Corporate/partner-with-us/developers-publishing/
Monetisation: Outright sale, rental or ad supported

Unfortunately, many of the portals do not reply at first, so persistence
may well be required.

Publishing on Steam

Steam is such a complex beast that I shall go into a fair bit more detail
than for the other portals. Let's start with the basics:
Website: http://store.steampowered.com/

Revenue Split: Negotiable
Contact details: Via Greenlight for new developers. It can be a very
difficult process to get onto Steam!
Monetisation methods: Outright sale and DLC

I'll be honest; I don't really like the approach Steam adopts with the
whole Greenlight process. I think it is a very negative way to try to get
a game onto a service; it can be very demoralizing for the developers
and it creates an overly competitive environment. Then there is the way
Steam does business: the secrecy, the dismissive responses to developers,
the closed-door approach. It reminds me of how the platform-holder
concept approvals used to be.

That said though, it is what it is, and if you want a successful PC game
you have to try to get onto Steam at some point. One very encouraging
bit of recent news is that Valve are looking to abolish Greenlight and
introduce a new, more open system for developers. In preparation for
this, Valve have ramped up the number of games they are Greenlighting,
and right now they are approving batches of 75 games every two weeks.

Flippfly recently published an excellent blog post highlighting the
challenges of getting onto Steam with their game Race the Sun, and how
important it is to make sure your game genre is compatible with the
Steam audience:

> The other thing we feel is a factor in our sales, is that we
> inadvertently shoehorned ourselves into the "Endless Runner"
> genre, without realizing the damage this would do. We felt the
> concept of an arcade-style, high-score focused game deserved a
> pure, HD treatment, free of micro transactions and with a focus
> on depth—and our customers seem to agree. But there seems to be
> an immediate and general stigma around this genre (thanks to the
> mobile revolution no doubt)—that "runners" should be free, and
> they don't belong on PC.
>
> (http://flippfly.com/news/race-the-sun-a-
> month-after-launch-losing-steam)

Once you launch your Greenlight campaign, you will get a whole load of
views and votes without having to do any promotion at all. The reason

for this is because your game will be automatically added to everyone's Greenlight voting queue. Alas, this will trail off after a few days and your traffic will rapidly drop. A good way to boost traffic is to take part in a giveaway via a large Steam group. Gift a certain number of copies of your game, while asking nicely for people to vote for the game. This can be a really effective way of getting quite a few more visitors and votes once the initial rush has tailed off.

To have a good chance of getting your game greenlit, you have to earn a large number of Yes votes. To really stand a chance of success you need to get your game into the Top 50 of highest votes, which can require upwards of 10,000 Yes votes. The current 'Average Top 50' split is 55% Yes / 45% No votes, with an average of 11,500 Yes votes.

One plus point is that there is no time limit, so you can run a Greenlight campaign in addition to your other sales activities, and just keep plugging away trying to increase the Yes votes. The general consensus on Greenlight seems to be that you need a thick skin, a lot of perseverance and maybe a good dose of luck.

A few more things to bear in mind for a successful Greenlight campaign:

Uses Images Within the Description

The description of your game is your shop window, and second in importance to the video trailer. Rather than stick with a block of plain text, keep visitor attention by inserting images into the description. To do this, add the line '[img]image url[/img]' into your game's description, and images will then appear within the description text.

Release a Demo on Your Site, Link It to Steam Greenlight

When releasing a demo of your game on your game and/or studio website, prominently link it to your Steam Greenlight page. A good demo can make a big difference to attracting visitors to your Greenlight page, and getting the all-important Yes votes.

If the Game Is Out, Link to it and Give Steam Keys Once Greenlit

If your game is already out elsewhere and available to buy, specify this and say that if you purchase the game now, you will receive a Steam key if the game is greenlit.

Jay Koottarappallil, of WhiteMoon Dreams, offers this advice following their successful Greenlight campaign for their game WARMACHINE: Tactics:

1. Launch the Greenlight campaign shortly after you start your Kickstarter. Constantly advertise between the two.
2. Just like Kickstarter, follow and handle the comments on your page.
3. Great screenshots are even more valuable on Greenlight than Kickstarter. People spend a lot of time looking at the text, video and rewards for a Kickstarter so there's a lot of content there. Greenlight only has text, which is less interesting than screens and video, so put work in that.

Once you have been successfully greenlit, you can then publish your game on Steam.

Insider Indie Q&A

1. *What is the name of your studio?*

   Yacht Club Games

Copyright © Yacht Club Games

2. *What year was your studio founded and what are the names of the founders?*

   2013—David D'Angelo, Ian Flood, Erin Pellon, Sean Velasco and Nick Wozniak

3. *What are the studio's key game titles?*

   Shovel Knight

4. *Do you have your own in-house engine or use a third party system? If third party, which one do you use?*

   In-house engine

5. *Which platforms do you release on now / plan to release on?*

We released Shovel Knight for Windows (Steam etc.), Wii U and 3DS. We're in talks to bring it to more platforms, but nothing is set in motion yet.

6. *Which is your most successful platform so far?*

Steam

7. *What are the development tools you use most (i.e. 2D, 3D software, audio tools etc.)?*

Visual Studio, Pro Motion, Photoshop, Famitracker, Illustrator

8. *What advice would you give to a new studio?*

Work hard and create deadlines that are realistic. Build something that you and the people around you love!

9. *What marketing resources do you use?*

None! We've generated all our own marketing. We built a list of 500+ emails, press contacts, YouTubers etc. that we message any time we have something we want to announce. At this point, we mostly try to announce things on our site, Twitter, Facebook etc. and hope people pick up the info and post it elsewhere without us lifting a finger (other than creating the original content ha!)

10. *What are your favourite indie games sites?*

TIGSource

11. *Any mistakes/hiccups you have made so far, something you would advise a new studio to avoid?*

We announced a release date before we were 100% sure we could hit it. I think it's a mistake to put yourself in a situation where you can disappoint your fans. Also, always be serious about financial planning and scheduling your time. A lot of making the best game possible is making sure your keep the scope and budget in line, so make sure to keep those elements in check so they aren't getting in the way of you creating a great game!

Publishing on the PlayStation Network

Registration websites
SCEE: http://develop.scee.net/software
SCEA: http://us.playstation.com/develop/

I have worked on various PlayStation systems over the years, including PS2, PSP, PlayStation Mobile and now PSVita. Sony's approach to working with small indie studios has changed a great deal over those years, and they are now the most progressive of all the platform holders.

The big change came with the PSP Minis program. We (Super Icon) published six titles on PSP Minis, and Sony of Europe were very approachable and a joy to work with. The Minis program offered regular monthly revenue in a far lower risk environment than a platform such as iOS.

As a European developer, one concern that I do have is that Sony of America is not particularly approachable. It can be very difficult for a European developer to get included in promotions. The best approach is to be patient yet persistent, and always try to remain friendly. Be prepared to be ignored, though!

Concept Approval

The concept approval process is now standardized across all of the PlayStation machines. It is a single stage process and products are now solely approved based on their scope and support of platform features.

Requirements

All titles are required to support one or more platform features, which are defined on the online submission form for each platform.

All non-exclusive titles must maintain feature and content parity with competing SKUs. Exclusivity is a three-month period.

Development Kits

Sony will, in certain circumstances, provide free loan development kits. If they like your game and want it on their platform you are very likely to get kits for no cost. If you do have to pay, while I can't give exact figures, a rough guide would be PS3 kits are under €2,000, PS4 kits under €4,000 and PSVita kits under €2,000.

Age Ratings

You must include the following age ratings for each title you submit:
► ESRB for North American release
► PEGI for Europe release

Translations

There is no requirement to provide a translated electronic manual.
For each title you release, the Metadata (PlayStation Store marketing description) needs to be translated into all of the languages for the regions you intend to release in. This can include:

- English
- French
- Italian
- German
- Spanish
- Danish
- Dutch
- Finnish
- Norwegian
- Polish
- Portuguese
- Russian
- Swedish
- Turkish

QA Submission

Sony are in the process of simplifying the QA process, so all regions will now only report Must Fix—'MF' and 'A' class TRC and Functionality bugs. You will have to fix the Must Fix issues, but any 'A' class bugs may be addressed at the publisher's discretion.

A word of warning—QA submissions can be a little inconsistent, so prepare yourself for frustration!

Product Codes

You get 400 free product codes for PAL territories and 400 codes for NTSC. These can be used for non-promotional uses (i.e. media, review, internal). Typically, you receive them within a week of your game release. You have to request them online though, so make sure you don't forget.

Financials

SCEE pay royalties on a monthly basis. They send you a statement, you invoice and payment follows a few weeks later. The revenue split is 70:30.

SCEA pay royalties on a quarterly basis. You don't need to invoice, and payment follows 60 days after the quarter end date. The revenue split is 70:30.

Pricing and Promotions

You set your own retail price for the PlayStation Store, and you have complete flexibility to alter this as you wish at any time.

Once you have a couple of titles on the PlayStation Store, you can start managing your catalogue. There are various things you can do such as 2-for-1 deals, multi-game bundles, price discounts on PS Plus and so on. You can time limit these deals if you wish and they can really help to boost revenues.

Sony often run their own special promotions, so try to involved in those. You will see a big increase in sales if you are part of a Sony promotion. Don't be too concerned if you have to drop the retail price for such promotions, the extra earnings will usually more than make up for this.

There is a lot of flexibility to keep earning revenue per title on the PlayStation Store, so you can really extend the long-tail.

Insider Indie Q&A

1. *What is the name of your studio?*

   hiive LLC

   "hiive" is a registered trademark of hiive llc.

2. *What year was your studio founded and what are the names of the founders?*

   2005, Andrew Rollings

3. *What are the studio's key game titles?*

   ▶ Creatures & Castles (iOS, Chrome, PSM)
   ▶ Zen Accumulator (PSM)
   ▶ Chromatic Aberration (PSM)

4. *Do you have your own in-house engine or use a third party system? If third party, which one do you use?*

   Both. We tend to prototype on an in-house engine and then rewrite portions of the underlying framework to target different platforms.

   However, this is an inherently inefficient approach so we are looking to switch to Unity in the very near future—particularly with the advent of their 2D tools.

5. *Which platforms do you release on now / plan to release on?*

   iOS, PSM (Vita), PC and possibly others in the future.

6. *Which is your most successful platform so far?*

   iOS, Chrome and PSM have all been similarly successful. We've more than broke even, but not by much. Enough to keep things ticking over nicely.

7. *What are the development tools you use most (i.e. 2D, 3D software, audio tools etc.)?*

   Visual Studio, Xamarin Studio, MonoDevelop, Photoshop, Audition, Paint.net, PSM Studio, TexturePacker. Pretty much the essentials.

8. *What advice would you give to a new studio?*

   Don't do it expecting to make any money any time soon, and don't give up the day job.

9. *What marketing resources do you use?*

   Marketing is something that I'm not very strong on and I need to improve in that area. Currently I use a mixture of Twitter, Facebook and Blog posts, along with contacting journalists that I've built up a relationship with over the years. I've never used any paid marketing resources, and honestly I'm unlikely to as I have an inherent dislike of the idea.

10. *What are your favourite indie games sites?*

    Probably indiegames.com or indiestatik.com

11. *Any mistakes/hiccups you have made so far, something you would advise a new studio to avoid?*

    Don't underestimate the value of polish, and don't leave it to the end of the project. Bake polish in from the beginning. If you put your game out without polish, the damage is done, and pulling back from that is difficult if not impossible.

    The first version of Creatures & Castles was not polished (as I had a limited time to develop it), and sales suffered because of it. If I was doing it again, I'd spend an extra month on polishing all of the rough edges out.

Publishing on Nintendo

Registration website
WarioWorld: http://www.warioworld.com/

Nintendo are much more approachable now, and finally seem to have gotten onboard with the idea of indie publishing. This has meant an end to the dreaded performance thresholds from WiiWare days, whereby Nintendo would only release your royalties if you sold several thousand units first. I still have a WiiWare title from a few years back that has never earned a penny, as it didn't hit the thresholds!

Concept Approval

There is no actual approval process. You have to submit a brief overview document, but unless there is objectionable content this is a formality.

Development Kits

Nintendo may, in certain circumstances, consider free loan development kits. If they like your game and want it on their platform, you may well be able to get kits for no cost. Again, I can't give exact costs for Wii-U development kits, but they are in the region of $3,000.

Age Ratings

You must include the following age ratings for each title you submit:
- ▶ ESRB for North American release
- ▶ PEGI for Europe release
- ▶ USK is also required for Europe release
- ▶ Australian release is optional, but if you do release there an OFLC rating is mandatory

Translations

You have to submit a translated electronic manual. Required languages include:
- ▶ English
- ▶ French
- ▶ Italian
- ▶ German
- ▶ Spanish
- ▶ Dutch

QA Submission

Allow for several weeks to go through the LotCheck process—Nintendo test quickly, but they stop testing once they find a handful of issues, so it can take many attempts to get through. Make sure your lowercase i's don't look like uppercase I's!

Product Codes

eShop releases receive 200 free game codes to send out to reviewers. If you need more than those 200 codes, you can buy more and these are charged at Nintendo's 30% cut of the sales price.

Financials

Both Nintendo regions pay royalties on a quarterly basis. You don't need to invoice, and payment follows 30 days after the quarter end date. The revenue split is 70:30.

Pricing and Promotions

You set your own retail price for the Nintendo eStore, which is a progressive step forward since the WiiWare days. You can also change the pricing at any time as you wish.

Nintendo also allow you to run time-limited sales promotions for your games, so you can finally develop a price strategy on a Nintendo digital download platform. Very good news indeed!

Insider Indie Q&A

1. What is the name of your studio?

Shin'en

2. What year was your studio founded and what are the names of the founders?

1999. The founders were Florian Freisleder and Manfred Linzner.

3. *What are the studio's key game titles?*

   Nano Assault Neo (Wii U), Nano Assault EX (3DS), Jett Rocket (Wii, 3DS), FAST Racing League (Wii, Wii U) and Art of Balance (Wii, 3DS)

4. *Do you have your own in-house engine or use a third party system? If third party, which one do you use?*

   We do everything in-house. Only for Physics we used recently BULLET, though a lot of changes were needed to get decent performance out of it.

5. *Which platforms do you release on now / plan to release on?*

   Wii U and 3DS

6. *Which is your most successful platform so far?*

   The most money we made on a game was on WiiWare. In general 3DS eShop is most successful. We also port our games for the Japanese market.

7. *What are the development tools you use most (i.e. 2D, 3D software, audio tools etc.)?*

   We use Maya for 3D, Cubase and Sony Soundforge for Audio, Photoshop for 2D.

8. *What advice would you give to a new studio?*

   Be smart and only make games that you are sure you can handle. We realize a game in 6–12 months. This reduces risk and keeps motivation high. We always work on more than one title. This allows us to shift work forces as needed instead of idling in certain phases of the project.

9. *What marketing resources do you use?*

   Twitter/Facebook and game websites that ask us for interviews and review our games.

10. *What are your favourite indie games sites?*

    Sorry, I don't know any. We like gaming sites like Nintendo Life and Nintendo Everything.

11. *Any mistakes/hiccups you have made so far, something you would advise a new studio to avoid?*

    Once we were signing a contract with a too low royalty. The game sold very well but we got only a fraction of the success. On the other side, this published game made a lot of new opportunities possible.

Publishing on Xbox

After an initial 'no indies' stance from Xbox for the Xbox One, they have now performed a full U-turn and launched the ID@Xbox self-publishing program for Xbox One. The program will "enable qualified game developers to build, publish and make their games available" without paying any application fees and with full access to the console's resources. Microsoft plans to ensure "easy discoverability" for indies via new trending and promotion features, and will give out two free dev. kits to registered developers.

A pretty good deal! Oh, and now they have also confirmed they will provide free Unity licences too. That's the kind of epic U-turn I like, so a big thanks goes to Microsoft for introducing the ID@Xbox initiative; well done, guys!

There is also a rumour that Microsoft will allow self-publishing on Xbox 360 Live Arcade in the near future. At the time of writing, nothing is definite, but XBLA certainly represents a huge potential audience, so this is interesting.

ID@Xbox

"ID@Xbox was crafted to ensure ALL developers can take advantage of this amazing platform, and the team met with more than 50 developers to hear what they want in a self-publishing program.

Developers will have access to the same great benefits that existing Xbox developers have today, including the full power of the console, cloud services, Kinect and Xbox Live toolset such as Xbox SmartGlass, multiplayer, Achievements, Gamerscore and more."

To apply to the program email id@xbox.com or complete the online form at http://www.xbox.com/en-us/Developers/id. Anyone can apply, but priority "will be granted . . . to independent game developers who have a proven track record of shipping games on console, PC, mobile or tablet."

Currently there are three possible responses you will get from Microsoft:

Not Just Now, but Keep in Touch
"This is not a 'no', this is a 'not right now.' We're evaluating the list of interested developers on a weekly basis and we will be in touch as soon as we're able to get you kits."

If you are a start-up without a well-known title or a track record of releases, this may well be the response you receive.

Tell Us More About You

"We'd like to ask you a few questions about your project . . ." You'll need to supply a design overview for the game(s) you would like to release on Xbox One. You also need to detail whether you are intending to use any middleware or development frameworks, and what platform specific features you are planning to support.

You're In!

The best response; an immediate yes. Once agreements have been signed, you'll have two shiny Xbox One development kits to play with.

Publishing on Apple

iOS Development

Official website: https://developer.apple.com/programs/ios/
Annual fee of $99

iOS development is incredibly easy to access and get started with. It is the single biggest factor in the many changes the games industry has gone through recently. Without iOS, developers would not now have the opportunities they do to self-publish on so many different formats.

That said though, there are downsides. It is very hard to make money on iOS due to the incredible over-saturation of the marketplace. Getting your game noticed is a battle, and it is a sad fact that most titles on iOS earn very little revenue. If you do happen to get a hit game on iOS you will see huge earnings, but be realistic before you begin, as that is the exception rather than the rule.

So, statistically speaking, the odds of achieving success on the App Store are tiny—and this applies to Android as well as iOS. Worse, the odds continually decrease with the many thousands of apps that are released on the app stores daily. Your chances of being discovered diminish every day, and that is a tough market by anyone's standards.

Right now it is really hard to offer any sound advice on how to make your game a success on the App Store; the best approach seems to be to experiment, ideally with more than one title. Try different pricing strategies, monitor your analytics closely, update your app regularly and always make sure that your mobile game is easy to learn and playable in short bursts.

Perhaps the most important aspect of mobile development is to choose your business model early on in the game design stage. A free-to-play game should be designed as such from the offset; don't try to retrofit free-to-play into a game as it just doesn't work. The available choices are:

▶ Premium
▶ Premium + in-app purchase
▶ Free-to-Play/Freemium
▶ Ad-supported

Make sure that you cultivate your customers over time, cross-promote, update your game often and provide value to customers.

And regarding free-to-play, perhaps I should explain what it is, just in case you don't already know (and I know you *do* know), but for the record:

Free-to-play (F2P) is a type of game that gives players access to a significant portion of the game content without the player having to pay. The most common approach is based on the freemium software model, whereby players are granted access to a fully functional game, but must pay micro transactions to access additional content or to improve in-game abilities or speed-up progress through the game. Often free-to-play titles require significant 'grinding,' whereby the player must spend many hours building up their progress, often quite arduously. This is where micro transactions then come in, to speed up this process and give access to the cool bits of the game much quicker. After all—most mobile gamers are busy people, and can't spend hours levelling-up.

Additionally, only a very small portion of players will actually pay anything for a F2P title. Right now approximately 0.15% of mobile gamers contribute 50% of all of the in-app purchases generated in F2P games, which is an incredible statistic!

Something like two thirds of the mobile market are F2P games, but it is interesting to note that there appears to be a swing away from F2P at the moment, and a resurgence of premium releases. Apple themselves are said to be keen to get more high-quality, higher-priced premium titles on the App Store right now. Bear in mind though that for a successful premium title you do need either a strong brand, or a very clear audience, or failing that a whole lot of luck!

The App Store details:
- You pick the price
- You get 70% of sales revenue
- Receive payments monthly
- No charge for free apps
- No credit card fees
- No hosting fees
- No marketing fees
- Volume purchasing
- In-app purchases
- iAd rich media ads

Sales and Promotions

Short-term sales can be very useful to increase sales and raise awareness for your game. The holy grail of app development is to get your game featured by Apple; you can expect massive sales increases if this happens.

A featured app listing only lasts a week so your goal should be to go as high in the charts as you can and then extend your popularity after the feature is over. Aim to start a sale towards the end of your featured week to close with a big sales boost, which should keep your app climbing up the Top lists after the featured listing has ended.

Free app weekends/days can also really boost users for your app, often massively increasing followers in a very short space of time. Wait until the app has been on the store for a while though (so price trackers will pick up the change).

Mac Development

Official website: https://developer.apple.com/programs/mac/
Annual fee of $99

As with PC publishing, you have a number of options you can pursue with Mac development. You can sell directly from your own website or use one of the game portals listed in the 'Publishing on Game Portals' section of this chapter.

Mac distribution actually offers you the chance to punch above your weight due to the relatively unsaturated market. It is much easier to get featured in a variety of Mac outlets, even with a smaller indie game. The Mac community can be a very friendly place, so make sure you take the time to engage with them as much as possible.

Mac App Store

From my own experiences, and those of other developers I have spoken with, games on the Mac App Store don't tend to generate much revenue. This is a shame, as it is a great store system, which isn't flooded with content.

What They Say

"The Mac App Store makes it easier than ever for users to discover, purchase and download your apps directly on their Mac. And with the Mac App Store available in over 150 countries, you can showcase your apps to millions of users around the world."

The details:
► You pick the price
► You get 70% of sales revenue
► Receive payments monthly
► No charge for free apps
► No credit card fees
► No hosting fees
► No marketing fees
► Volume purchasing

Insider Indie Q&A

1. *What is the name of your studio?.*

Psydra Games LLC

Psydra Games LLC

2. *What year was your studio founded and what are the names of the founders?*

   ► We founded Psydra Games LLC in 2012. The founders are:
   ► Alex Gold: Designer and Project Manager
   ► Jim Otermat: Coder
   ► Joe Kelly: Coder and Audio
   ► Kyle Perry: Business, PR and QA

3. *What are the studio's key game titles?*

   We have only released one title so far, Dark Scavenger, though we are working diligently on a new game.

4. *Do you have your own in-house engine or use a third party system? If third party, which one do you use?*

   We developed Dark Scavenger in Flash and we're using Unity for our new project.

5. *Which platforms do you release on now / plan to release on?*

   Dark Scavenger is currently available on PC and Mac. Since we are building our next title in Unity, we should have plenty more platform options next time around.

6. *Which is your most successful platform so far?*

   PC has been our most successful platform by far.

7. *What are the development tools you use most (i.e. 2D, 3D software, audio tools etc.)?*

   Since Dark Scavenger was a 2D Title, we were able to build it completely in Flash and code it in FlashDevelop. Art was created in Adobe Photoshop and Audio was handled through Reaper, Cubase and Studio One.

8. *What advice would you give to a new studio?*

   Make something that you're passionate about. You're not doing yourself or the video game industry as a whole any favours by re-treading old ground. Without passion, your product is going to emerge droll and lifeless.

   Branching out as an independent developer means that you have the freedom to make something that you want to make, unburdened by the weight of a client's requests. Take advantage of it!

9. *What marketing resources do you use?*

   Marketing resources we use:

   ► Social media: There are plenty of social media sites but in my experience, Twitter and reddit are the most useful.
   ► Twitter is a great way to communicate with fans and network with other developers. Also, a lot of game journalists use Twitter, making it easy

to get in touch with them. Reddit is a massive social media site where the right post can get thousands of eyes on your project. Every game developer should post on /r/gamedev and participate in the weekly Screenshot Saturday and Feedback Friday threads where developers can show off what they're working on and get constructive feedback. A lot of press people pay attention to Screenshot Saturday on reddit and the hashtag #screenshotsaturday on Twitter.

▶ Press list: We created a massive press list by collecting the contact information of every gaming website we could find.

▶ Also, the website http://www.pixelprospector.com/ was incredibly helpful with this and with other game development things as well.

▶ Games Press: Whenever we have a major announcement, we send a press release to http://gamespress.com, which a lot of game journalists use to find stories.

▶ Bundles and pay-what-you-want sales: These are a great way to get your game into the hands of thousands of players, but are best utilized when your game has been out for a while. Bundle In A Box, Indie Game Stand and Indie Royale are a few of the good ones.

10. *What are your favourite indie games sites?*

IndieStatik is our favourite indie games site. They cover both small and large-scale indie gems and are the first to break the scoop on upcoming titles.

11. *Any mistakes/hiccups you have made so far, something you would advise a new studio to avoid?*

Don't over scope your games! While having passion is a necessity, getting carried away with it can lead to overblowing the budget and timeframe. It's the easiest mistake to make and the most difficult one to recover from.

Dark Scavenger originally was going to be episodic. We planned to release the first episode for free and then craft additional episodes down the road depending on the success of the first one. Somewhere down the line however, it got into our heads that the story worked best when taken in as a whole, driving us to finish all five planned parts before releasing the game.

Although it was the right decision for the game overall, the amount of work required to get us to that point nearly broke us. Several people dropped out over the course of the project due to its length, causing us to cycle through almost twelve different artists. There were also several breakdowns both on the code and design side; a few of us swore that we would never make a game again!

Now that it's all over, I don't think any of us have regrets but we certainly learned a lesson about getting over-zealous.

If we had more experience as a team, we may have been able to handle the project more gracefully, but given that it was our first time working together, our lack of cohesion almost did us in.

Long story short: Be passionate, but also be reasonable. The longer your project drags on, the more likely it is that people are going to drop off. Make sure you can finish what you start!

Publishing on Android

The first thing that you need to realize with Android publishing is that there is a lot of choice. Many different systems use the Android OS, so you can publish on Android phones, Kindle Fire, Nook, OUYA, GameStick and more. Right now it seems a new Android powered device is announced every week!

Like the iOS, the Android marketplaces can often be heavily over-saturated. Additionally, as Android is so open, piracy is a big problem. It can be very difficult to earn decent revenue on Android, although as with iOS, if you do get a hit the numbers can be very good indeed.

Let's start with the various Android stores that are available:

Google Play

Website: http://developer.android.com/distribute/googleplay/publish/register.html
Registration fee: $25
Revenue split: 70% (developer) / 30% (Google)

Google Play is the primary App Store for Android. This will most likely be your first port of call when publishing an Android title.

Amazon App Store

Website: https://developer.amazon.com/welcome.html
Registration is free
Revenue split: 70% (developer) / 30 (Amazon)

The Amazon App Store is the next largest App Store for Android after Google Play. If you develop an Android title, you definitely need to release on Amazon in addition to Google Play.

SlideME

Website: http://slideme.org/developers
Registration is free
Revenue split: 70% (developer) / 30% (SlideME)

For most developers SlideME is either second behind the official
Android Market for global distribution or third for US distribution
behind Amazon App Store. It is also slightly different from either in that
it is a community and content driven marketplace, uniting developers
and users. Many developers, particularly smaller ones, have actually
reported better sales on SlideME than on Google Play, so you should
certainly consider releasing your Android games on SlideME.

What They Say

"SlideME offers products, services and experience that help promote
small Android developers and their creative efforts, without locking
them into any closed standards. We are focused on addressing and
helping developers gain quality assurance and financial rewards in this
exciting multi-billion dollar industry.

Have an application that you wish to distribute to more than 50% of
Android devices without Google Play or Google prevents you from
stocking in Google Play, leaving you and your app stranded? Are there
users desperate to buy your application but they don't have access
to Google Checkout or Google Play? Do you want to show off your
app but feel limited by not having what you need in the Google Play
Marketplace?"

Amazon Fire

Website: https://developer.amazon.com/appsandservices/solutions/
devices/kindle-fire
System price: Various
Revenue split: 70% (developer) /30% (Amazon)

There are now several Amazon Fire devices available, include the Kindle
Fire tablet, Fire smartphone and Fire TV set-top box. These are Android
powered devices, and the good news is that 75% of Android apps tested
just work as-is on Kindle Fire. You can also distribute HTML5 apps on
Kindle, so you have various options available for Fire app creation.

Amazon are really keen to get new game content onto their devices, and are running various promotions to encourage this, including free Amazon coins to qualifying apps.

The Amazon developer console is a big plus point for Fire development, it is one of the most fully featured consoles around and it allows easy access to your stats, analytics and promotions.

Below I have highlighted a few of the key features available to developers on Amazon:

Appstore Developer Select

Appstore Developer Select helps get your qualifying mobile and HTML5 web apps discovered and gives you more opportunities to boost your sales and revenue. As a developer with one or more qualifying apps, you will receive the following benefits:

▶ Enhanced Merchandising to Improve Discovery: We'll provide enhanced merchandising for your apps that are live in the US, UK, Germany, France and Spain via dedicated Amazon Appstore home page placements in each of these countries and consider your apps for advertising on Kindle Fire. Additionally, your qualifying apps that are live in the US Amazon Appstore will receive 500,000 free mobile ad impressions across the Amazon Mobile Ad Network.

▶ Amazon Coins Rewards to Customers to Improve Conversion: Consumers purchasing your app or in-app items in your app will receive up to 30% of the purchase price back in Amazon Coins.

▶ 25% off Amazon Web Services to Help You Scale: You will earn 25% credit back on qualifying purchases of Amazon Web Services (AWS) products, up to a maximum $500 credit per year.

Free App of the Day Program

The Free App of the Day (FAD) is a curated promotional opportunity, where Amazon offers one paid app to customers free each day. Participation in FAD helps you gain greater exposure and drives significant traffic to your app. The apps we select are featured in some of our most visible marketing placements, including placements on mobile devices, Kindle Fire, and the Amazon Gold Box Best Deals page, and are complemented by social media exposure including a Facebook post and Twitter tweet. These placements and the exposure they provide drive significant traffic to the featured apps and allow the developers to grow their installed base quickly.

Developer Promotions Console

Want to run a 24-hour special holiday sale or discount all of your mobile apps to celebrate the launch of a new game? It's easy! Developer Promotion Console gives you a quick and easy way to create temporary discounts for your mobile app and mobile in-app items.

As you can see, Amazon are taking indie game development very seriously, and it is definitely one of the best Android options right now.

OUYA

Website: https://www.ouya.tv
System price: $99
Revenue split: 70% (developer) / 30% (OUYA)

Since its 2012 *Kickstarter* campaign, OUYA has generated a lot of interest from indie developers. It has a low barrier of entry and cost-effective kits and offers mobile gaming in the living room.

OUYA is an open platform with very good developer support. The storefront has an easy to use interface and is curated well, with various logical product categories and special spotlight categories. There are not too many games on the OUYA site (500 at the time of writing), so visibility for your game can be very good.

Unfortunately not many OUYA users actually bother to buy games, they tend to just play the free versions. Emulation is also very popular on OUYA, with many OUYA owners playing games via emulation as opposed to buying the store games.

GameStick

Official website: http://gamestick.tv
System price: $79
Revenue split: 70% (developer) / 30% (GameStick)

GameStick is another *Kickstarter* success story, but differs from OUYA in that it takes the form of a HDMI stick with a separate controller.

You simply plug the stick into an HDMI port on your TV—minimal wires—and go.

What They Say

"Portable, Dynamic, Revolutionary: Introducing the world's most portable TV games console. Launch your favourite Android games in full HD and rediscover your love of play!"

An open system with a very low hardware price. At $79, GameStick is $20 less than OUYA and offers unrivalled portability. Unlike OUYA, players can buy games directly from the storefront. GameStick has no free component requirement, although you can still release freemium titles if you wish.

There are certain basic standards that GameStick games need to follow, such as specific resolutions/aspect ratios, an average framerate of 25 fps, and so on.

Nook

Website: https://nookdeveloper.barnesandnoble.com
Registration is free
Revenue split: 70% (developer) / 30% (Barnes & Noble)

NOOK's singular approach to merchandising unlocks the potential of high-quality apps that go underserved in other stores. Apparently, if you release on NOOK they will deliver unmatched opportunities for discovery, exposure and sales.

Note: You require a US (EIN) Employer Identification Number before you can register. See Chapter 9 for further details.

Partnering With Games Publishers

Another approach to publishing is to go through a publisher, which can certainly help get your game noticed. In particular, many of the mobile publishers have a huge reach and range of cross-promotion options that most developers can only dream of.

My personal feeling is that teaming up with a decent publisher is definitely the best way to get featured on the various app stores and maximize revenue from a game, particularly with a first title.

Publishers often have extensive marketing resources, a wealth of PR contacts and good contacts with the various distribution networks. I would say though that you should only consider the bigger publishers, those with the largest reach, or the smaller ones that have been recommended by other developers. Never trust your game to a publisher you don't know.

Devolver Digital

Website: http://www.devolverdigital.com/games/page

What They Say

"Compact and powerful, our team of industry veterans and pioneers possess the knowledge, resources and passion to turn projects of all sizes into a smashing success. Whether your project needs our help from the initial concept phase, or it just needs a good kick in the pants on its way out the door, we are here to help."

Midnight City

Website: http://midnight-city.com

What They Say

"Modelled after our favourite record labels, Midnight City provides promotional, production and business service and support for independent game developers."

Thumbstar

Website: http://www.thumbstar.com

What They Say

"Thumbstar is a global digital developer, distributor and publisher of mobile games and apps. We work with independent developers all over the world and publish in the UK and Europe, S.E. Asia, the Americas, Middle Eastern and Australasian markets."

Ripstone

Website: http://www.ripstone.com

What They Say

"If you want a publisher that shares the same indie spirit as your studio then we'd love to talk to you. Ripstone does everything you'd expect from a traditional publisher, but with a twist. We believe indie devs need a more tailored, personal approach to their games and that the relationship between developer and publisher is the difference between a game that is merely good and one that is great."

Chillingo

Website: http://www.chillingo.com

What They Say

"Chillingo, a subsidiary of Electronic Arts, is a leading games publisher on mobile platforms with numerous award-winning hits around the world including Angry Birds, Cut the Rope, Contre Jour and Iron Force. The company also publishes games for Android, Windows Phone 8, Steam and other digital platforms."

DotEmu

Website: http://www.dotemu.com/en

What They Say

"Established in 2007, DotEmu licenses, converts, publishes and distributes beloved retro games on today's market."

Points to Consider When Approaching a Publisher

Revenue Split

The percentage of revenue split between you and the publisher will vary from publisher to publisher, but try to keep it as low as you can. Some will go as low as 20–30%, others will try to insist on 50%. Always negotiate—the stronger your game proposal, the more leverage you will have to negotiate. The ideal scenario is a near finished game that has already generated positive interest from the games press and your followers.

Payment Terms

Once the publisher receives the revenue from the distributor, how long will they then take to pay you? You need to specify a time frame within the contract, and try to agree as short a time as possible. Anything over 30 days is excessive.

Intellectual Property Rights (IP)

KEEP THEM, always. Never give up your IP. This is the value of your business.

Ports to Other Devices

The publisher may try to get the rights to handle conversions to other formats if you don't want to develop for those systems. Avoid this—you would end up having to give all of your source code and art, and you lose control of your product.

What Will They Do?

Ensure the contract specifies exactly what the publisher's responsibilities will be; what is their marketing plan/budget, what is their PR plan, will they cover translation costs if need be, will they help with QA, and so on. If it isn't specified, you will have to do it and cover the costs.

One Final Thing

A footnote here, I actually asked several publishers (including mobile publishers such as Ripstone, Chillingo and Thumbstar) for quotes to include within this section of the book, on how they can help indie game studios. They either didn't respond, or promised to put something together but never did.

The cynic in me worries that it is the same old game publisher mindset, can't be bothered to reply, 'too busy' etc. Hopefully that isn't the case and they would actually be super-responsive to studios that reach out to them, but I thought it was worth mentioning.

Post-Mortems

Life of Pixel—Our First PC and Mac Launch

Over at Super Icon, our latest release is Life of Pixel, which is the first game we have launched on PC/Mac. It has been a learning experience, and has taught us a lot!

We launched Life of Pixel via the Humble Widget off our own website, http://www.lifeofpixel.co.uk. This was followed by a release on Desura. As a team we have put everything we can into Life of Pixel, dedicating not only time, but 30 years of gaming love and affection.

What Is Life of Pixel All About?

Life of Pixel is a retro delicacy dedicated to the brilliance of classic gaming machines and groundbreaking game favourites. You play as

Pixel, the inquisitive little green hero on a quest to explore where pixels began life. Follow his journey through video game history by collecting the bit-gems and unlocking each amazing game machine. Collect the 'Specials' and unlock more! Armed with awesome power-ups, Pixel must vanquish the enemy pixels and bosses who try to thwart him throughout his quest.

Take a journey with the wizened Professor Pixel and revisit the golden age of gaming. Featuring a massive variety of beautiful pixel art from classic 8- and 16-bit game systems, such as Amiga, SNES, Mega Drive, Commodore 64, Apple II, Game Boy, NES, Atari 2600, ZX Spectrum and Master System!

Look out for nudges to console classics like Mega Man, Castlevania, Zelda, Streets of Rage, Shinobi, Metroid, Wonder Boy, Pitfall, Sonic and more. Revisit computer legends such as Turrican, Uridium, Jet Set Willy, James Pond, Rick Dangerous, Prince of Persia, Impossible Mission, Exile and lots more.

With over 100 fun-packed levels of platforming goodness! Chock-full of tricks and traps, double jump challenges, gravity inversion, special power-ups and loads of different enemies.

Life of Pixel Is Go!

We eagerly launched Life of Pixel and contacted the press to let them know about our amazing new game, asking them to have a play and hopefully cover and review it. Unfortunately we made a major error of judgement here, and failed to sufficiently promote the game before release.

It has been an uphill struggle to gain interest in Life of Pixel— particularly to get reviewers to take the time to review the game. Right now the PC indie market is saturated with indie games; getting that all-important break and attracting attention for a new PC title is getting harder and harder.

The other issue we have encountered is a slight backlash towards retro platformers, particularly those that, like Pixel, lack combat. The 8-bit retro aesthetic has been done to death it seems. Additionally, as we focused so heavily on the vintage console/computer systems, going back as far as early machines like ZX81 and Atari 2600, many people just didn't get that. Many (most?) indie gamers weren't even born in those early days, so they have no affinity with those systems. They are more familiar with the modern slant on retro gaming, such as Hotline Miami, Super Crate Box, BroForce, Mercenary Kings, and of course—those games are all combat heavy.

Sales Figures Since Launch

So let's look at the figures . . .

From our own site we have sold 54 units since the launch, and on Desura we have sold six copies so far. This is far less than we expected, but it goes to show that it is a tough market!

The reviews that we have had so far for Life of Pixel have been mostly positive, including a 9 out of 10 from CultNoise Magazine. So the question is—what is going wrong, why aren't we getting sales or coverage?

As mentioned above, our big mistake was not enough development hype and coverage while we were developing Life of Pixel. For all future games, we will blog extensively throughout development, reaching out to our followers and press alike. We will also broadcast live development videos on Twitch. It isn't all doom and gloom though for Pixel, we are now starting to get a little more coverage, particularly with YouTubers, and we are continuing to promote the game heavily, and also to run competitions, giveaways and sales.

We also launched a Steam Greenlight, and at the time of writing, we are 42% of the way into the Top 100.

Feelings So Far

Life of Pixel is my baby, my concept and project. I have been shaken by the poor sales and general lack of interest in the game. In my darker moments I worry that I have got it wrong; is Life of Pixel pointless rose-tinted nostalgia that no one is actually interested in? Is it too British, too difficult, is it lacking content? Is there, honestly, no market for such a game? Has the indie bubble burst on PC/Mac?

Perhaps this is the single, hardest and most brutal of all lessons that you can learn as an indie developer—that your game isn't going to do as well as you hoped, no matter how good a game you think it is. But there is always that glimmer of hope—the hope that if you do keep trying to get the word out, that one day your game will get noticed by someone who can make a difference. At times it feels like you are holding out for a lottery win, or some other random-based occurrence, but in many ways that is the life of an indie game developer. The best indie game in the world still needs a little luck to get it noticed.

I feel that everyone should play Life of Pixel—it is special; unique yet fun, a wealth of content and secrets to discover, a sense of adventure and plenty of gameplay twists and turns. A game with charm and a voice of its own!

What's Next for Pixel?

We are indie, so we have used our strengths as a small, adaptable team and over the last few weeks we have devoted a whole lot of work into various tweaks and refinements to Life of Pixel, and added a lot of new content. We've made all machines (bar the secret machines) unlocked from the beginning, adjusted the difficulty in places, reduced 'cheap deaths' where we could find them, added a camera look-up/down feature and several new gameplay mechanics. We have added three all new 16-bit machines; Amiga, SNES and Mega Drive, plus lots of new enemies and game features such as new traps, buzzsaws, trampolines, skateboards and minecarts to ride, planes to fly, cannons to shoot Pixel, power-up potions and bombs, switches and puzzles, and many more additions.

We act on user feedback and reviewer comments and we make a better game. We listen to input from other developers, we share our story—all these things help to turn a negative into a positive. So, even if we don't manage to improve sales, to reverse Pixel's fortunes, we still learn a huge amount of very useful stuff, and all the new knowledge goes towards making our next game more of a success. This is indie development!

Our Android Console Experiences So Far

Releasing on OUYA

There is a lot to like with many of the Android consoles, I use my OUYA on a daily basis and I really like so much about it. As such, it seemed a good idea to develop a game for OUYA, to test the water and see how it would perform.

Brick Break Blitz seemed a good fit as we had a game partway through development, which would lend itself well to the OUYA. OUYA also supply a Unity extension, so you can go from Unity to console relatively painlessly.

The development process was straightforward enough, after a little fiddling the Unity to OUYA pipeline was set, and one really great feature is that you can transfer builds to the console via Bluetooth. One oddity we did encounter was the controller input lag, we never found out if it was the Unity extension at fault, or a glitch with the OUYA, but sometimes controller input would lag behind the onscreen action. The result of this was that you couldn't control the game for a frame or two, which was really frustrating.

We did quite a bit of press for the game, but it was difficult to get coverage, as the game was just a traditional brick breaker. We kind of expected that, and truth be told we only chose to do a brick breaker as a quick test project for Unity. Still, we got quite a few positive ratings and we were featured within the 'Play Like BAWB' section. We made the game free-to-play, as was originally compulsory for OUYA titles, with a free 10-level episode to download and then the option to purchase three more episodes, comprised of 75 new levels.

The numbers were poor though, and at the time, we compared notes with many other OUYA developers who also reported low-ish numbers. So, after a few months on the store, the current figures stand at:

Downloads: 1520 units
Purchases: 56 IAP units
We earned around 70% per sale, so $78 total revenue. I am sure you will agree those numbers are terrible! As a result, we decided not to release anything else on OUYA.

Kindle Fire TV
Our next foray into Android console development came courtesy of Amazon. They had seen Brick Break Blitz on OUYA, liked it, and asked

if we could convert the game to the (at the time) upcoming Kindle Fire TV. It was all very top secret, and exciting—we had never released a launch title before.

Amazon lent us a development kit, and provided a Beta Unity extension, so we could export from Unity to the device. The conversion itself was nice and easy; as Fire TV was also an Android console, not many changes were needed. The main addition was adding Amazon Game Circle support, but that actually didn't take long—just a little trial and error at first.

We completed on time, and were really pleased to have hit the launch window. We kept the same pricing and free-to-play model as the OUYA version, as Amazon liked that approach. We also got quite a bit of 'free' coverage as part of the Amazon launch announcements, which was nice. Unfortunately, that is where the good times ended!

The conversion/purchase rates were appalling, even worse than OUYA! And again, other developers I have spoken to encountered the same sort of poor figures. So here we have, drum roll, our Kindle Fire TV stats to-date for Brick Break Blitz:

Downloads: 3,514 units
Purchases: 51 IAP units
We may still try our hand with another title on Fire TV—after all, it IS Amazon—but we would certainly look at a different pricing structure.

In conclusion, Amazon consoles are a tough market—there are developers out there who have sold reasonable numbers, but they are certainly the exception rather than the rule. At this moment in time I would recommend focusing your efforts more toward PC/Mac, iPhone/iPad, Android phones and traditional consoles.

The Indoor Pub Games Sports World PlayStation®Vita Post-Mortem

Our first Vita development experience, Indoor Sports World, has been an interesting one. Financially it has been a bad experience, so many months of development all funded by not taking any wages. Developing a Vita engine, along with a fairly large game (it may seem simple but there is a lot of stuff in Sports World).

It has also been a really good learning experience, and it has forever changed my approach to development. No more developing and maintaining our own engine, trying to support new platforms and features. From now on it is third party all the way, using development systems such as Unity.

What Went Right

Focusing on Solid Graphics Performance in Our Engine

We spent a lot of development time working on our game engine; adding effects and graphical touches and making sure they ran at a decent framerate. We looked very closely at the graphics effects in the Vita game 'Hustle Kings,' as this seemed to be the game we would most likely be compared to. We wanted our game to look as nice, if at all possible, and I think we managed to get close.

We added real-time reflections for the balls, so you can see the scene properly reflected on each ball. We also added a normal map to the ball surface to show slight damage/chips to the enamel of the balls. It is a slightly different approach to how the balls were rendered in Hustle

Figure 2.1 Shiny balls!

Kings, but I was pleased as I didn't want to directly copy their approach, and I feel this gave Sports its own identity.

Next up were the other environment touches, such as nice reflective floors, water reflections, decent specular mapping and real-time shadows. I was the sole artist on the project, and as such I wanted to make each and every environment look as realistic as possible. My other aim was to have lots of variety within the environments, so they all looked very different from each other while still maintaining a level of believability—so you could expect to find such places in the real world.

I used normal mapping combined with real-time reflections to try to make the various surfaces look realistic and interesting. One incredibly useful tool I used for the job was ShaderMap, initially version 1, and later version 2. I tried Crazy Bump too, but preferred the extra control and lower price of ShaderMap. I used quite a few textures from CGTextures, and as none of them come with normal maps I had to create a lot of these from the textures, which is where ShaderMap came in. The key was to increase the detail on the generated normal maps; smoothed normal maps look horrible—like plastic wrap on everything. I also made sure the maps weren't too intense, otherwise you get some nasty sharp edges in there where the light changes are too extreme.

Figure 2.2 Nice lights and shadows

The other real-time effects we experimented with were real-time SSAO (Screen Space Ambient Occlusion)—which is a rendering technique for adding subtle shadowing to all the nooks and crannies in the meshes, and Bloom. Bloom is the effect of light bleeding out from very bright areas, giving a subtle glow to the scene if used right, or a sticky coating of grease if overdone. Unfortunately, we couldn't get these two effects running fast enough, and decided, as they were only minor details, to drop both in favour of a solid framerate.

The final element for each environment was light baking; to render each environment with realistic lighting and shadows with minimal performance overhead. Our implementation works by a sort of reverse ray trace. It takes each pixel, works out what lights are visible from it; taking into account type of light, distance and light colour etc., and works out a lighting value for the pixel. Many of the scenes included dozens of lights added to provide a nice range of lighting and shadow variation.

So all in all a lot of time and effort went into making the graphics look as good as possible, to make each environment as immersive and believable as possible.

Adding Plenty of Detail in the 3D Artwork

There's not much point spending time developing graphics effects if you don't have plenty of scene detail to utilize those effects. As such I really tried to add as many details and touches to each environment as possible. I used quite a few pre-built assets from sites such as Turbosquid and Dexsoft, for elements like furniture and fixtures and fittings. I found some amazingly good stuff on there—I think my favourite assets were the leather sofas from the Brewery Pub venue. I love those sofas!

The base scenes are about 20–30,000 polys (a mixture of quads and tris), the balls are several hundred each, the tables and dart boards another few thousand. Texture resolution was mostly 512 × 512, with the odd 1024 × 1024 texture in there on larger areas. Smaller detail bits were OK with 256 × 256 or even lower res textures.

I was surprised how much geometry detail and how many textures the Vita could handle. To be honest I expected to have to cut detail down a fair bit, but in the end I didn't really have to compromise at all.

Plenty of Game Modes and Rule Sets

We tried to add a nice variety of different game modes, and rule sets for each of the games. While you always want more, I think we got a decent level of variety in there. I'd have liked online multiplayer, but it was just impossible given the resources we had (we are a two-man team; Steve on code and myself on art, design and audio). The offline multiplayer works well, and seemed a nice compromise.

We also tried to include plenty of unlocks and rewards, for customising the various game equipment such as play tables, cues, darts, boards etc.

While we only included one Air Hockey mode, Steve spent a lot of time optimising to ensure that Hockey ran at 60FPS, which is essential to the smooth flow of the game.

What Went Wrong

Developing Our Own Tech

Historically, we have always developed our own tech; supporting several console platforms such as PS2, PSP and Wii. It seemed a natural progression to continue this and expand to Vita; can't be that difficult, eh? Well it was tough: Chuck Norris tough. The Vita is great and the development environment is first-rate, but poor Steve just had too much on his plate. The task was huge, particularly as we had never added shaders into our engine before. All the new graphics effects were added from scratch. We ditched the old routines for things like specular and environment mapping, and rewrote them all to take advantage of what the Vita offered.

It all just took so long, Steve working silly hours adding to and adapting the engine. Even features like video playback and audio took a lot of time to get right and smoothly integrated into the engine. It was a killer—during this time we were not earning any money, it was all just one huge ever-increasing expense. Our release windows kept sailing by—we had originally planned to launch Sports (or Pub Games as it was originally named) shortly after the Vita launched!

Looking back, I think we needed two or three engine coders to handle a task like this, but then without income, that was just not possible. Also, the Vita just isn't as powerful as say a PS3 or Xbox, so it required a fair few months of code optimisations to get decent performance out of the various shaders and effects. When we first added the various new effects, the game ran at about five frames per second!

The Game Was Too Big

It seems silly to say it, given the impression most people have is that the game is very simple. However, it is true, this is one big game! There were so many modes to keep track of, and the Arcade and Season modes take hours to fully test.

This is the odd thing with sports games; they seem simple but in fact are really difficult to properly test and balance due to the time it takes to play through modes like Season and Career. Add to that developer familiarity and you have a situation where you really need some fresh eyes and external QA support. We didn't have the budget for this unfortunately, and it let us down.

Not Enough Testing Time

I hang my head in shame and admit Sports needed more testing. The difficulty isn't properly balanced; it gets too hard, too quickly. As touched upon above, Steve and I were both so used to the way Sports plays that we were able to beat opponents that in hindsight are stupidly hard. The game is about amateur indoor sports, not professional sporting prowess.

Figure 2.3 My favourite venue—Bar16Bit

It really needed an extra period of testing, testing and more testing. The other issue we had was that by the end of the project we were beaten, financially and morally. No money to live on and a sense that this game would never be finished if we didn't get the bloody thing out quickly. I've had some tough development experiences in the past, but I think this was in many ways the most damaging. It just felt like it would never end, and when all your money goes, you get evicted from your house and have to sell your personal stuff just to buy food, you know you are doing something badly wrong!

TRCs and Sony QA Submission

Sony TRCs (Technical Requirements Checklist) are in short, a complete and utter nightmare. Again, I really feel for Steve, I think his head actually melted at one point due to the extreme levels of pedantry associated with implementing the TRCs. There are just so many eventualities and scenarios you have to factor in to properly implement the TRCs. Also we tackled many of these at the end of the project, when we were both heartily fed up with the whole thing.

Sony QA was an exercise in frustration, too. When you desperately need to start earning money from the game, hitting QA is akin to running into a brick wall. The testing process is slow, and each resubmission adds a few weeks to the time it takes to get the game out. In total, it was about two months or so of back and forth with QA before we were approved. One particularly frustrating round was the one where they only found one single issue, a MF (Must Fix) bug, which they found on day one of testing. 10 days later they concluded the testing with no more bugs found. Yay, we thought, quick fix and we're sorted. We resubmitted with the fix, and then on day one of the resubmission QA found one new MF issue, then no more.

Steve and I were convinced by this point that Sony hated us, and they were never going to let Sports get through!

What We Have Learned

First and foremost, never to attempt to develop our own tech again. I think that you need to be a fair bit larger than our two-man team to effectively develop and maintain your own cross-platform tools and technology. You also need plenty of financial support in place to keep things ticking during the R&D phase.

To ALWAYS give more time to testing. We made mistakes here and it has cost us in review scores and user goodwill.

We also released a patch to rectify certain issues, primarily:
- ▶ Tweak the AI, as Darts and Air Hockey are exceptionally hard to beat on later levels
- ▶ Fix Darts issues; sometime it is too easy and sometimes seemingly random
- ▶ The player's finger obscuring the darts and pucks at times on the front screen
- ▶ Add aiming aid for Pool and Snooker back into Arcade Mode
- ▶ We always try to fix mistakes/hiccups if we can; user feedback is really important to us and one of the best bits of development.

Conclusion

It is time to move on, and leave sports titles behind—I fancy a change! In my career to date I have developed eight Pool/Snooker games, a PSP Darts game, two Bowling games and two games with Air Hockey included. They are always very test heavy, and not the sort of games to ever really get good press coverage or build up a community.

From this point on, I shall be focusing on original, unique games such as Life of Pixel. Games that I can really get my teeth into and implement something special. With the exception of my first Unity test game, this is the direction Super Icon will go from now on.

A PSP Minis Adventure

This is an older post-mortem, but I have included it here as we learnt a lot of valuable experience from our PSP Minis publishing days.

PSP Minis were a range of smaller, cheaper downloadable games for the PSP and PSP Go. Minis were limited to a size of 100MB or less.

We developed and self-published a total of six PSP Minis:
- ▶ Arcade Air Hockey and Bowling
- ▶ Arcade Darts
- ▶ Arcade Pool and Snooker
- ▶ Bashi Blocks

- ▶ Family Games
- ▶ Golf Mania

We also released three different bundles, which were various combinations of the above titles for a reduced price:
- ▶ All-in-One Sports
- ▶ Arcade Sports Bundle
- ▶ Massive Minis Collection

We released our first PSP Mini, Arcade Darts in July 2010.

Prior to this we had developed and self-published several WiiWare titles, which was a fairly stressful experience thanks primarily to Nintendo's performance thresholds which required a minimum number of sales before you started to receive royalties. Ah, those were the days!

Working With Sony

The PSP Minis program was a breath of fresh air. Sony promoted the service well, you could update your games if you needed to once they were live, control the pricing and participate in the many pricing promotions Sony ran on PSN. Sony were very approachable and very developer friendly, they even loaned us the PSP dev-kits. This is something Sony still do now; they often lend 'loan' systems to developers, particularly PS Vita and PS3 development kits.

I had heard a number of horror stories about the low sales numbers for Minis before we started, but we were pleasantly surprised. Certainly compared to the bigger console digital download formats such as XBLA and PS3 PSN and high-selling iOS Apps, the numbers were quite low—but looking back now the figures seem really good. You also knew with certainty that each new Mini released would generate a few thousand sales, allowing business and cash flow planning that is often not viable on platforms like iOS, where sales expectations can be rather unknown.

Another huge positive was that Sony Europe paid royalties monthly, which they still do now. Oddly, SCEA do things completely differently, paying quarterly (plus 45 days from end of quarter).

Bundles and Promotions

As mentioned above, we released three different Minis bundles during the long-tail sales period. These were really easy to set up, we just selected the games, decided on a name for the bundle and wrote the marketing text required for the PSN Store. The interesting thing here was that even though the games had been out quite some time by this point, the bundles earned nearly as many sales as the original games. Having a catalogue of game titles you can actually do this sort of promotion with is hugely beneficial, as you can see some really good increases in overall sales revenue. The other interesting thing we found was that the individual games that were now part of the bundles still continued to sell, with very little decrease in their sales numbers. Incredible, really, looking back.

PS Plus

We also ran several PS Plus promotions, such as a discount off the game price, or free game offers (buy one, get one free). These often resulted in a huge sales surge for the duration they ran (which was usually a month).

Facts and Figures

PSP Minis sales have a seriously long tail; we still earn revenue from them now, after all these years! Our biggest sellers sold around 30,000 units, which compared to our recent releases on PC and Android seems amazingly good now.

Insider Indie Q&A

1. What is the name of your studio?.

Gushiku Studios

Gushiku is the Okinawan word for 'castle'. I'm also a martial artist, so the name comes from that aspect.

2. *What year was your studio founded and what are the names of the founders?*

My studio was founded in 2011 so it's relatively young. I'm the sole founder—this is a one-man operation.

3. *What are the studio's key game titles?*

The very first title I put out is named DB42, which utilizes teleporting mechanics like what you see with portal. I've also got a couple of pub-style slot machines out there as well: Necro Brainz for the zombie lovers, and Toyland Slots for the Christmas crowd. My most recent game, released to Google Play on Nov. 2, 2013, is named Dragon Swoopers. Dragon Swoopers is a platformer-based flying game where the object is to fly a dragon around a level, collecting eggs, gems, coins . . . as well as capturing or destroying sheep and cows.

4. *Do you have your own in-house engine or use a third party system? If third party, which one do you use?*

All of my games use Bad Logic Games' freely available libgdx framework. You get sound, UI, graphics and physics engine capabilities from that. On DB42, I used Tiled for level building. Dragon Swoopers saw use of the RUBE editor for physics-based level development. The underlying architecture in Dragon Swoopers also uses Spine for sprite animation and the Artemis Entity System Framework for object handling.

5. *Which platforms do you release on now / plan to release on?*

So far all of my releases have been based on the Android and iOS mobile platforms. The distribution channels (i.e. app stores) make publishing extremely simple.

6. *Which is your most successful platform so far?*

By far my most successful platform would be Android. Development and publishing through Google Play and Amazon have been pretty easy and straightforward.

7. *What are the development tools you use most (i.e. 2D, 3D software, audio tools etc.)?*

I've used a variety of tools in my games:

- ► Tiled: level development
- ► RUBE: level development and physics handling
- ► Spine: animation (adds significant polish to the game with an INCREDIBLY USEFUL animation editor)
- ► Box2D: physics engine included with libgdx
- ► Audacity: sound handling
- ► Gimp: raster graphics editing
- ► Inkscape: vector graphics editing (INVALUABLE!)
- ► Eclipse: project development

- ▶ Artemis: object modelling
- ▶ Universal Tween Engine: simplified interpolation handling and timelines for animation

8. *What advice would you give to a new studio?*

About the best advice I can give is to keep in touch with other developers. This can be either through web forums or what have you. It's been through this constant contact that I've been able to learn new things and add extra polish to the games I've worked on.

9. *What marketing resources do you use?*

I've got my own website, GushikuStudios.com, that I post development info on. I also use Twitter, YouTube, Facebook, reddit and developer forums.

10. *What are your favourite indie games sites?*

I really like http://forums.indiegamer.com/forum.php for contacting artists. Otherwise, I hang out on http://www.badlogicgames.com/forum quite a bit.

11. *Any mistakes/hiccups you have made so far, something you would advise a new studio to avoid?*

The biggest difficulty has been trying to avoid the 'delusion of grandeur.' I was certain that I was going to make millions with my first game, DB42. That didn't materialize. It also didn't materialize with any of the subsequent games that I developed. So far, it's been pretty much all beer money. But, staying true to the dream of making it big keeps you going.

CHAPTER **3**
QA, Localisations and Age Ratings

QA Bug Tracking

Traditionally the domain of the publisher QA department, one of the major time-sinks with self-funded development, is testing. If you have limited resources, try to test as you develop—the more ongoing gameplay testing and tweaking you do, the better the end game will be. Test, balance, tweak, polish and test some more!

Added a new feature? Test it thoroughly before moving on; make sure it works and works well. The worse thing to do is to leave testing until the end when you are getting tired of the project, perhaps a little burnt out—how could you possibly give the game the play testing it deserves in that scenario? Your aim should be to focus on how a game plays from the early gameplay stages.

There are a few other reasons why it's important to fix bugs now rather than putting them off until after Alpha:
- ► Bugs are often quicker to deal with the sooner they're dealt with, as the code is fresh in the mind.
- ► If you implement a feature and then test it until it is bug free and playing right, you know you can rely on that part of the game to perform well.

► Crash bugs can slow down adding new features because if the game keeps crashing, it can slow down implementing all other features of the game. There is nothing more frustrating than trying to design levels in a game that often crashes.

► It's harder to implement features that work and play well if the underlying implementation is bugged. Aspects such as player control, movement and interaction can never be properly balanced if the code is not solid.

Key to your entire bug fixing efforts is the process of tracking those pesky bugs. In the initial stages notes in a pad may well be sufficient, but don't delay setting up a solid bug tracking system. So what is bug tracking?

Bug Tracking Software

A bug tracking system is a software application that is designed to help keep track of reported bugs. You can add issues, mark them as fixed or send them back to the developer if they are not properly fixed.

Ideally this should be an online database (some systems require you to run your own servers), and look out for extra functionality such as companion iPhone apps, so you can test and note down bugs on the move.

A typical bug tracking process is as follows:

Add an Issue
Here the developer adds a new issue. The issue does not have to be programming related, it can be a problem found in the levels, graphics, audio etc. The circumstances of the bug and steps to reproduce it are included in the report. Often including a screen-grab of the issue in action can be a big help, or even better a video reproducing the bug.

Assign the Issue
After adding an issue, it must then be assigned to the team member responsible for that aspect of the project. Once the bug is assigned, the individual is sent an email with the bug information, along with a link to the bug on the tracker.

Set the Priority

Each bug is given a priority ranking, from urgent must-fix bugs down to suggestions that can be waived if it isn't deemed important or is a 'feature.' This ensures critical bugs are fixed first.

Verification

After the assigned developer fixes the issue, the tester then verifies that the bug no longer occurs. In some cases bugs may be marked as features (i.e. not a bug) and closed.

So let's take a look at a few of the most popular bug tracking solutions out there. I have only included the free or cheaper options, as there really isn't a lot of point in a smaller indie studio paying upwards of $20 per month for bug tracking.

Bugzilla
Website: http://www.bugzilla.org/
Price: Free

Bugzilla is a 'Defect Tracking System' or 'Bug-Tracking System.' Defect Tracking Systems allow individuals or groups of developers to keep track of outstanding bugs in their product effectively. Most commercial defect-tracking software vendors charge enormous licencing fees. Despite being 'free,' Bugzilla has many features its expensive counterparts lack.

Mantis
Website: http://www.mantisbt.org/
Price: Free

MantisBT is a free, popular web-based bug tracking system. It is written in the PHP scripting language and works with MySQL, MS SQL and PostgreSQL databases and a webserver. MantisBT has been installed on Windows, Linux, Mac OS, OS/2 and others. Almost any web browser should be able to function as a client.

There is also a mobile app for iPhone, Android and Windows Phone which allows you to track and log bugs on the move. The price for the mobile app is $50.

Trac
Website: http://trac.edgewall.org/
Price: Free

Trac is an enhanced wiki and issue tracking system for software development projects. Trac uses a minimalistic approach to web-based software project management.

It provides an interface to Subversion and Git (or other version control systems), an integrated Wiki and convenient reporting facilities.

I have used Trac for all of our bug tracking for the past few years. It is very reliable and does the job well. It can be a little fiddly to set up, but once you are up and running it is easy to maintain.

GoPlan
Website: http://goplanapp.com/
Price: $10 per month for the 10-user/project Starter Package

GoPlan lets you keep track of your projects and collaborate with your colleagues securely through an intuitive user interface.

Jira
Website: https://www.atlassian.com/software/jira
Price: $10 per month for the 10-user Starter Package

JIRA is the tracker for teams planning and building great products. Thousands of teams choose JIRA to capture and organize issues, assign work and follow team activity. Many game studios use JIRA, most likely because there is an additional Agile package, which includes Scrum and Kanban project management tools. The 'Pro' choice!

Working With External QA

If your budget stretches to it, there are QA companies out there who can assist with the bug tracking process, but they can quickly become very expensive. Shop around and find a good one to work with that won't break the bank—often a single test round can cost in the thousands, and to make it worthwhile you will need more than one round of testing.

You will have to manage any external QA carefully, so first and foremost make sure to only get the QA Company involved when the game is ready (i.e. feature complete and internally tested). Keep a close eye on how they are spending their time; I actually heard that one QA company tried to charge for their testers sitting around waiting for a build! Also bear in mind that the QA companies are running a business to make money, so they will push you for extra test rounds that may not actually be necessary.

Always make sure when you supply builds that you send along clear Build Notes. Detail what is open for testing, list any known issues to avoid and be very specific.

There are various different types of testing that are offered, including:

Functionality Testing

Generally, it focuses on improving the quality of video games from the player's viewpoint. Functionality testers hunt for all issues pertinent to gameplay including but not limited to:
- Crashes
- Game mechanic issues
- Level flow issues
- User interface functionality
- Testing the game's stability
- Ensuring correct scoring
- Game performance
- Game asset integrity

Compliance Testing

Compliance testing is the process of testing a game to ensure that it meets the rules and requirements set out by the console manufacturer, i.e. Sony publishes a Technical Requirements Checklist (TRC), Microsoft publishes Technical Certification Requirements (TCR), and Nintendo publishes a set of 'guidelines' (LotCheck). More often than not you will have a build failed on one or more of those issues, so the more you address before platform holder QA, the smoother and quicker the submission process will be.

Example of compliance issues include:
- Making sure the game handles things properly if the controller is disconnected

- ▶ Save devices used properly
- ▶ Network packets aren't encrypted
- ▶ All standardized text (error messages, info messages etc.) are correct
- ▶ Correct usage of proprietary logos
- ▶ Ensure saves can't be copied between profiles
- ▶ Make sure achievements can't be won by cheating

Compatibility Testing

Compatibility testing is normally required for PC titles, near the end of development. They check whether or not the game runs on different configurations of hardware. The hardware could include various brands of CPUs, video cards, sound cards, and input peripherals such as gamepads, joysticks and other components. It will also evaluate performance for the game's minimum system requirements.

Usually two rounds of compatibility tests are performed—the first during the Beta test phase, and the second just before the release candidate is ready.

Testing Companies

I have only included companies with a good reputation within the industry, and again, be aware that costs can run into the many thousands:

Babel Media
Website: http://www.babelmedia.com/
Contact: info@babelmedia.com

EC-Interactive
Website: http://www.ec-interactive.com/
Contact: Via online form

Localsoft
Website: http://www.localsoft.com
Contact: info@localsoft.net

Testronic
Website: http://www.testroniclabs.com/games/overview
Contact: Via online form

Triple A Testing
Website: http://www.tripleatesting.com/
Contact: info@tripleAtesting.com

VMC Game Labs
Website: https://www.vmc.com/games/
Contact: info@vmc.com

Language Translations

There are various degrees of localization. If you are self-publishing on an open format such as PC you have the easy option of no translation of any sort, while releasing games on consoles often requires compulsory text translation for things like store text and electronic manuals. There is never any compulsory requirement to translate in-game text, although you should consider the benefits that this may bring. It can certainly help when trying to promote your game in foreign speaking regions, but if you have a lot of text and a number of languages this can be very expensive.

One thing is for sure, if you intend to release on consoles you will need to arrange for language translations. Make sure you find a good, low-cost translation company that you know provides a fast turnaround and a reliable service. I've had a few occasions where I have needed translations done for a promotion within a couple of days; fortunately, we use a great translation company (Rangeela) and they always deliver on time.

The first thing you'll learn is to write everything fairly concisely. When you are paying for translations, wordiness will cost you! Make your manual text lean and efficient, although leave enough info in there to still make it useful. If you are careful with word count you can bring an EFIGS&D e-manual in at under $500.

So, where to go? There are a fair few translation houses out there, but to make life easier the list below includes only the ones I have received personal recommendations for. It is worth noting that it really is best to go to a company specializing in games translations, as they will be familiar with the TRC/LotCheck terminology requirements.

Translation Companies

Rangeela BV
Website: http://www.rangeela.nl/
Contact: info@rangeela.nl
Note: I heartily recommend Rangeela, having used them for all my translations over the past few years.

Babel Media
Website: http://www.babelmedia.com/
Contact: info@babelmedia.com

Localsoft
Website: http://www.localsoft.com
Contact: info@localsoft.net

Partnertrans
Website: http://www.partnertrans.com/
Contact: info_uk@partnertrans.com

SimulTrans
Website: http://www.simultrans.com/
Contact: info@simultrans.com

Universally Speaking
Website: http://www.usspeaking.com/
Contact: info@usspeaking.com

Age Ratings

Depending on your release platform(s), you may be required to get ESRB (US), PEGI (Europe), USK (Germany) and OFLC (Australia) ratings.

For the home console downloadable services you will need to obtain age ratings for each of your games. It is a very straightforward process, the only hassle being that it (in some cases) costs money. Boo!

An interesting recent development is that PEGI has announced the formation of an International Age Rating Coalition. This new system will be deployed as a single online form, which developers and publishers complete to generate a rating for their product. Instant product classification at no cost, as the various platform holders will cover all costs. These global ratings are operational now, but the platform holders haven't yet finalised their storefronts to support them.

Keep track of updates on their official site:
▶ https://www.globalratings.com

The participating territories include the UK, USA, South America, Australia, New Zealand and Brazil amongst others. Once fully implemented by the various platform holders, this should cut out the European and Australian age ratings costs completely—which is very good news indeed!

For now though, you will need to contact each ratings board in turn. First off, you should register and set up an account for your company:

PEGI
Website: www.pegi.info
Contact: deboer@nicam.cc

ESRB
Website: www.esrb.org
Contact: mhochheiser@esrb.org

USK
Website: www.usk.de
Contact: schulz@usk.de

AGCB
Website: www.classification.gov.au
Contact: accounts@classification.gov au

To do this just drop them an email and they will send the necessary forms. Once that is done, you will have access to the publisher areas on their sites, to which you can submit a product for rating. Using a downloadable game as an example, I have detailed the process for each of the ratings boards below.

The Ratings Process

PEGI

Complete the online submission form. You must then send them a copy of the game along with the fee (in this case the casual game fee of €250). You should also include a 10-minute gameplay video, a selection of screenshots along with the game manual to cover all bases. Within 10 working days, you should receive your rating.

USK

Download and print the submission form. You must then send a copy of the game along with the fee of €1200. You should also include a 10-minute gameplay video and a selection of screenshots along with the game manual. The examination will be completed within 15 working days.

AGCB

Download and print the submission form. You must then send a copy of the game along with the fee (in this instance, Level 2, AUS $890). You should also include a detailed written description of gameplay, a separate recording of any contentious material in the game and typical gameplay footage. A classification decision will be made within 20 working days after the application has been recommended to the Board.

ESRB

A lot has changed over at the ESRB recently, and they are now the most progressive ratings board for small studios. For a download only title (e.g. Xbox Live, Nintendo eShop, PlayStation Store, PlayStation Mobile, Windows 8, PC download, websites) you complete the online form, submit it and receive an instant rating for no charge. If only all ratings were this straightforward!

CHAPTER 4
PR and Reaching Out to the Press

Before you start to engage with the press, you need to get together an attention grabbing overview of your game. The purpose of this is to sell your game to the press and game players alike; it should include the various aspects that make your game special. Detail what makes your game stand out, why they should play it and what they should expect. It is a good idea to keep the tone more conversational than corporate—you are an indie developer, so show the love for your game.

Aim to get the overview right first time—hopefully attracting some press interest, and more importantly, players to your game. If you get it wrong, if you fail to put the message across about why your game is special, you could well find that you actually put people off your game before they even try it. A badly done overview could even deter fans of the type of game you are creating, your natural 'tribe', and you really don't want to do that!

Always challenge your assumptions and consider what the appeal of your game concept is from the perspective of your audience. It is very easy for a game developer to become very isolated, to lack the objectivity to properly convey the message of their game. If you can, ask other people for their feedback on your overview before you go live. Never rush this stage, take the time to get it right, it really is worth it.

So where to begin? Generally most game descriptions include the following aspects:

► Game icon
► One sentence to describe the game, the 'hook'; you need to sell the game in this opening line
► A descriptive paragraph describing the game in further detail
► Closing line and call-to-action for the player
► A bullet-point feature list describing up to five of the very best, and most unique, features of the game
► Marketing keywords

Let's look at each of these in turn . . .

Game Icon

The game icon is the first thing people will see of your game in any online store. The design may vary from store to store—some icons on the PC stores are more like banners, but it has to look amazing!

It has to look as eye catching and professional as any icon in the top charts of your chosen online stores. A good trick is to prepare a mock up and compare your icon with other icons for similar games, particularly the most successful examples—your icon has to look every bit as good, if not better, than those other games. Don't just try to copy other game icons, you run the risk that people will perceive your game as a cheap clone, jumping on the bandwagon.

Once the icon is designed, get friends and family to look at it to gauge their feedback and opinions. If they don't immediately say it is fantastic, then tweak it or start again. It can be a good idea to prepare more than one icon, and compare them to each other and ask opinions on which looks best.

Make sure that the icon is legible at small sizes; it is usually best to avoid using words in your icon, and don't clutter your icon with free or sale messages.

Tagline—A One-Sentence Description of the Game

The tagline needs to highlight what makes your game unique and what key aspect will attract players to your game. You could use a tagline that describes the unique gameplay of your game, one that sums up the nature of the gameplay. As a player, if you were to read this one line, would you read further? Would it entice you into giving the game a try?

If you haven't got a strong hook for your game, how can you market the game and expect people to take notice? Why would anyone play your game?

Patrick O'Luanaigh, CEO at nDreams, had this to say over on the GamesBrief (http://www.gamesbrief.com) website:

> I'm a big believer in 'the hook' (I think EA used to call it the 'razor X'), a one-line description of your game that explains why it's unique and will grab attention from the plethora of games out there. It's similar to Seth Godin's fantastic 'Purple Cow' concept—making sure your game will stand out and has a reason why people will notice it.
> Too many games don't have that hook. Without it, your marketing is utterly crippled.

Descriptive Paragraph Describing the Game in Further Detail

This is the essentials of the description, the primary marketing tool for players who are interested in learning more about your game. This is your chance to tell the player exactly why they need to own your game. What makes your game fun? What are its unique aspects and how will it engage them? This should tell them what the game is about, so it is crucial that this paragraph is clear and interesting.

Keep it concise but exciting and make sure you tell the player what they will get to do in your game. This is also the ideal place to mention any awards your game has won, or to detail good review scores.

Closing Line 'Call-to-Action'

A call-to-action (usually abbreviated as CTA) is a line of text (or it can be an image) that prompts your visitors, leads, and customers to take action. It is, quite literally, a 'call' to take an 'action.'

You have to give the reader a compelling reason to do what you want them to do, or there is no way they are going to click that button. Use actionable language—speak directly to the reader, and use active verbs. Action-oriented verbs directed to the second person (you) consistently perform well in CTAs. Action verbs also make the copy shorter, giving you a more effective and concise call-to-action. The objective is to get the reader to do something immediately, so make it good! A few action verb examples include Buy Now, Get It Now, Download Now, Immediate Download.

Last, write your text in the active voice rather than the passive, i.e. where the subject does or 'acts upon' the verb.

Bullet Point Feature List

Make sure each item on this list sounds exciting and explains how that particular feature enhances the player's enjoyment of the game. These points are about the fun aspects of the game, the things that make the game so special. These are your unique selling points—the points that make your game rise above the competition.

Bullet Point Basics

The following is a set of rules to follow that will help you write good bullet points:

1. Convey a clear game benefit and a promise of something good to the reader. Try to encourage the reader to revisit the meat of your content, or go straight to your call-to-action if it is that good!
2. Try and keep your bullet points symmetrical; meaning, one line each, two lines each etc. This makes it easier for the reader to follow.
3. Avoid clutter in your bullet points. Your bullets should be designed for clarity; there should never be any confusion with the presentation.
4. Apply 'parallelism' and keep your bullet groups thematically related. Try to maintain the same grammatical form within each bullet.
5. Bullet points, like headlines, don't need to be full sentences.

Marketing Keywords

Often before anyone finds your game they will have performed a search, particularly on the mobile app stores where there can be hundreds of thousands of games and apps. The keywords that you select for your game need to match those that the user types into their search criteria. If your keywords match their search terms in some way, your game will be listed somewhere in their search results. Keywords are the most important marketing tool you have at your disposal on the various app stores, so take the time to get them right. You should also track and monitor their performance after release.

Your app title is also very important here, and should be used in conjunction with your keywords. Keep the title human-friendly, but keyword optimized and remember that the title works together with your keywords in the searches.

Depending on the store you are selling on, there will be a character limit on the number of keywords you can use. The Apple App Store, for example, limits you to 100 characters, including commas and spaces. Spaces after commas are not necessary and you don't need to add your app name into the keywords.

It can be a good idea to try to use current popular terms or trends in your keywords, providing they are relevant to your game. There are a few online tools that can be really useful in helping you to decide upon and track the performance of keywords in your game, and to compare your keywords to those in other games on the App Store. The examples below are unfortunately all iOS only, but I am sure such tools will become more readily available for other platforms:

AppCodes
Website: http://www.appcodes.com

Perform App Store SEO, track your competitors, check out popular keywords, dispense your apps' promo codes effectively.

SensorTower
Website: https://sensortower.com

Track your app's individual keyword rankings, get up-to-date alerts on your app's position both for individual keywords and in the Featured and Top 1000 list, and optimize your keywords automatically to improve their efficiency.

Full access to SensorTower is a little on the expensive side, but even if you can't afford one of their pricing plans you can still check out the keywords for other apps, and find out a whole load of other details all for free. Just enter an app name in the keyword search box on the main page and it will list the keywords that app uses. By way of example, apparently Angry Birds uses the following keywords:
sky, angry, puzzle, fun, action, cool, physics, birds, egg, pig, slingshot, center, destruction, genial, cerdo

You can also compare your keywords directly with keywords from other games. The next bit is even better: click on the app icon for the game you just searched. This takes you to an information page that includes various details on the app, such as estimated worth (i.e. revenue earned). Very useful and seems quite accurate. Referring back to our Angry Birds example, the original version is worth $8,158,630!

Insider Indie Q&A

1. *What is the name of your studio?*

   The Chinese Room

2. *What year was your studio founded and what are the names of the founders?*

   As a mod team, 2007; as a professional studio, 2011

3. *What are the studio's key game titles?*

   Dear Esther, Amnesia: A Machine for Pigs, Everybody's Gone to the Rapture

4. *Do you have your own in-house engine or use a third party system? If third party, which one do you use?*

Third party. We've used Source, HPL2 and currently we use CryEngine.

5. *Which platforms do you release on now / plan to release on?*

PC, Mac, Linux. Right now, PS4 and we're also gently playing around with Android and iOS.

6. *Which is your most successful platform so far?*

PC

7. *What are the development tools you use most (i.e. 2D, 3D software, audio tools etc.)?*

The usual—Maya, Photoshop, Visual Studio, plus the third-party engine.

8. *What advice would you give to a new studio?*

Finishing is a lot harder than starting—make sure you schedule a proper amount of time for it. Check your budget and get advice from someone who understands development costs so you don't sell yourself short in terms of studio costs—things like PAYE or middleware can be a nasty shock if you didn't plan for them. A good lawyer and accountant will pay for themselves within the first year, so get one. Understand your market and talk to your community all the time. Don't give up and don't make something you don't believe in 100% because it's hard, so you need that passion. If it doesn't work out first time, don't be discouraged. Most studios struggle at first; be in it for the long game. Treat the people you work with and alongside both in the studio and wider contacts with professionalism and respect.

9. *What marketing resources do you use?*

Mainly it's been personal contacts with journalists. Twitter, a website, these are essential. Getting the game out and visible at festivals and things like that can be really powerful.

10. *What are your favourite indie games sites?*

Rock, Paper, Shotgun. Not really indie, but a really good-quality threshold on the writing.

11. *Any mistakes/hiccups you have made so far, something you would advise a new studio to avoid?*

Yeah, we didn't clock how difficult and time consuming running a business on a day-to-day level was if it's not what you are good at. We left it too long to get a manager, an accountant, a lawyer, and it cost us in terms of time, stress and money. If you don't have those skills, getting someone good in will make a massive difference to both your output and your personal life.

Copywriting Tips

In the past, I have written a number of very dull game descriptions and press releases, full of boring words and features. It is actually really hard to come up with good, sexy copy that will leap off the page and sell your game to the player. The golden rule is to always remember that you are *selling* a game, not describing one, so make sure you use words sparingly and avoid dull words and phrases.

Learn by Example

Scour the App Store and read the descriptions of the top-selling games. What makes them sound exciting? Do they sell the game to you? You should hopefully see that every sentence highlights a reason why the player would want to play the game.

Make note of the phrases and points that most strike you, learn from those game descriptions. Often the bigger and more successful titles have benefitted from the services of a professional marketer/copywriter. Use plenty of exciting genre-specific words that jump off the page such as action-packed, fast-paced, thrilling etc.

Start Sentences With Action Verbs

An action verb is a word that expresses doing something, that gets the reader straight into the action, immediately describing the player's role. They can be particularly effective if used at the beginning of a sentence and are often the main verb of a sentence, e.g. run, jump, fight, reach, chase, catch, dodge etc.

Here's a nice example from the game Cubic Creatures:

"Slide, Stack and Crack your way to victory in this CLEVER Addictive PUZZLER!"

The link below includes a very useful list of action verbs, many of which are ideal for game descriptions:
► http://www.websavvy.com.au/a-list-of-action-verbs-to-use-in-your-ads/

Use Active Voice

Verbs in the active voice can really help to bring life to your description. Writing in the active voice means constructing sentences where the subject acts, such as this example from Rovio's Angry Birds:

"The survival of the Angry Birds is at stake. Dish out revenge on the green pigs who stole the Birds' eggs."

Economize Your Words

Wordiness is distracting, so be concise. When you streamline your wording, your message becomes more powerful and clear. Removing excess wording can give your text more clout. Try to never waste your readers' time and remember the golden rule: less is most definitely more.

Limit Jargon

Jargon is language specific to certain groups and as such is not appropriate for more general readership. While you do occasionally need to use a little jargon, try to use plain speaking, ordinary language whenever you can. Too much technical language can quickly alienate the reader.

Keep Sentences Short

The Gunning Fog Index formula is often used to measure the readability of text. The underlying message is that short sentences written in plain English achieve a better score than long sentences written in complicated language. Gunning believed that 16 to 20 words was a good average word count for sentences in newspaper articles, but for something like a game description or press release, 12–16 is more optimal.

Press Releases

The points above also apply to a good press release, but there are certain other specifics a press release requires. First and foremost, keep it short, with five paragraphs at most in the body of release. A press release should never exceed a single page in length.

Another important thing to remember, particularly from an indie standpoint, is the style of wording you use to compose the release. Try to show your excitement for the game in your writing, but keep it casual, personal and humorous (if you can). Avoid dry, corporate sounding text, which can be a big turn off for the press. You are an indie developer, not CEO of a multi-national! Don't be too worried if you can't convey humour well in writing; excitement and enthusiasm for your game can be all you need.

A Good Press Release Needs a Good Headline

Editors are usually swamped by emails and press releases, so they are far more likely to open an email with a headline that grabs them. An effective headline is your main chance to get an editor's attention.

Famed copywriter and ad man David Ogilvy once said, "On average, five times as many people read the headline as read the body copy. When you have written your headline, you have spent 80 cents out of your dollar."

Here are some tips:

▶ **Keep it short.** Aim to bring your headlines in under 70 characters, and try to include at least one keyword. A great headline can be spoken in one breath.
▶ **Watch your tenses.** Effective headlines usually involve active voice and strong present-tense verbs. You can also use future-tense when the headline describes future events.
▶ **Use ordinary language.** No complex words or jargon phrases, you are appealing to the person in the street and they need to understand what you are saying. Vivid, simple language grabs attention.
▶ **Title case.** Press release headlines should be written in title case. When using title case, do not use capital letters for prepositions (such as in, on, at, of, for) unless one is the first word.
▶ **Subheading.** A subheading is optional, and is meant to encourage the reader to read the press release further. The press release headline, subheading, and first paragraphs should mimic each other. To summarise, the first paragraph is an extension of the subheading, which is a more verbose way of stating the headline.

First Paragraph

This paragraph should tell the journalist and reader what the press release is about. There is a good chance that a game writer would skip over your press release if the information you present in this paragraph is not interesting and concise.

The first paragraph (two to three sentences) should sum up the press release, and the additional content must elaborate it. Your headline and first paragraph should be written so that they stand alone, i.e. if they are the only parts of the press release quoted, the release still makes sense.

Second Paragraph

Here you can add detailed information about your game in order to support the first paragraph. Focus on the game's key features, unique selling points, game story and the inspiration for the game. Avoid dull techie phrases such as high-polygon, real-time rendered, physics-based; instead, emphasise what makes the game fun to play.

Last Paragraph Call-to-Action

Sum up your game or story and go straight to the point of the press release.

Examples:
"The Early Access version of YourGame is now available on Steam. Download now from http://store.steampowered.com/yourgame"
"Get YourGame now for 1.99 GBP from the App Store on iPad, iPhone and iPod touch or at www.AppStore.com."

Assets
Provide links to the game/assets here, such as review codes or links to download the app, screenshots, videos, company or game website, Facebook page, Twitter account. Check out the 'Press Kit' section below for full details.

About Your Studio
The final paragraph should describe your company. You can also mention any relevant awards you have won and other key games you have released.

Media Contact Information
Include your contact information; such as first and last name, email address, telephone number, LinkedIn address, and any other relevant contacts. A Skype number can be a good idea, as international phone calls can be expensive.

Make sure you emphasise that you welcome questions, interviews and such; let the press know that you are accessible.

Important Points to Remember

Be Professional

Excessive CAPS, exclamation points or typos will ruin your credibility. Proofread, spell check, then proofread again. Silly mistakes will kill your press release.

You Are Writing for Journalists

Press releases are not intended for consumers; they are for journalists who will often use them as a starting point for a piece. Avoid using promotional or marketing language; journos HATE sales-type releases.

Why Should Anyone Care?

Make sure your press release is newsworthy; focus on the elements of your release that make it stand out as something new and noteworthy. The human touch can be a good angle; an interesting team story or company milestone achievement could really help to get more interest.

Targeted Pitching Can Be More Effective than PR 'Blasts'

If possible, identify who might be interested in your particular style of game, check the sort of games they cover and have reviewed most highly. Try to make the release intro personal to them and their site, introducing them to the game and trying to get them interested. If they like your game they could become an evangelist for your game amongst the media, which is a fantastic thing as it really helps to boost your visibility.

The Press Kit

A Press Kit (also known as a Media Kit) contains a collection of images, videos and additional information about the game and the developers. A great tool you can use to put a Press Kit together is presskit():

"presskit() (pronounced 'do presskit') is the solution. Free for everyone, open and easy-to-use for both developers and press. Developers only have to spend an hour or so creating well laid-out press pages with everything the press needs to write to their heart's desire. Everybody wins." Download from: http://www.dopresskit.com.

Press kit contents:
- ► Company Bio
- ► Press Release
- ► Fact Sheet
- ► Logos
- ► Banner Art
- ► Screenshots
- ► Videos

Let's look at each of these in turn.

Company Bio

This should contain more information about your company and list the principals/founders of the studio, along with a concise background on each person.

The bio should list the games your company has made; don't worry if this is your first game, just be honest and say that it is your debut title. You can also mention any relevant awards you have won.

Press Release

Include your launch press release, with a full description of the game.

Fact Sheet

Facts about your game, including:
- ► Game description
- ► Key features/USPs in bullet point form
- ► Game genre
- ► Release date
- ► Price point in USD and EUR
- ► Available platforms
- ► Direct download link on iTunes/Steam
- ► Developer name and link

Logos

Company and game logos in various different sizes. Try to make two versions in both 72dpi (for computer screen) and 300dpi (for print) resolutions. Include the App icon and game logo with alpha channels.

Banner Art

This is optional but it does make it much easier for journalists to integrate your art if you use the IAB (Internet Advertising Bureau) display standards. You should aim to include the following banner sizes:

300 × 250 pixel—Medium Rectangle
300 × 600 pixel—Half Page
728 × 90—Leaderboard
468 × 60—Banner
120 × 600—Skyscraper
160 × 600—Wide Skyscraper

Screenshots

A selection of your best screenshots, with human-readable filenames, and all viewable online. Include a link to a zip archive of all images. People often look at images before they read the text, so make sure your screenshots show that the game looks fun. Try and get plenty of action shots, rather than the hero sitting there doing nothing.

You can also add text within each screenshot, which can be a good way to get key features across to the viewer. You see this sort of approach a lot on the various mobile app stores.

Aim for 10–15 good solid shots of your game. You can also create exclusive shots for your preferred journalists.

The sizes should match the resolution of each of your target platforms (i.e. iPad 2 1024 × 768, iPhone 4 640 × 960, iPhone 5 640 × 1136, Vita 960 × 544 etc.)

Avoid standard menu screens such as the Main Menu and Options Menu as no one wants to see these. The Title Screen is OK to include.

Videos

Often screenshots and descriptions just aren't enough to get the press interested in your game, especially within the overcrowded mobile market. A good quality video can be the most important thing you can use to sell your game to the press—who may well decide if they are interested or not based on the promo video.

Your video should show what the game is all about, highlighting fun looking gameplay segments. It should clearly show your USPs; what your game offers that others don't.

Between one and two minutes is the ideal length to hold your audience's attention. The first few seconds of a trailer can be the most important to capture the viewer's interest, so make them special!

Music and sound effects are essential to set the tone of the video. A good soundtrack can make a trailer stick in the mind long after the viewer has watched it. A great example, and one of the best movie trailers ever, is John Carpenter's Halloween: http://www.youtube.com/watch?v=T5ke9IPTIJQ.

Even now, it makes the hairs on the back of my neck stand up. The soundtrack is incredibly effective, immediately drawing you in. It is so good you want to see the film without even watching the visuals! Avoid copyrighted music tracks though!

Be sure to include download links to higher quality versions, as certain outlets prefer to upload the video to their own servers and media channels. Include review quotes and scores if you have some good ones.

End your video with a call-to-action. Direct the viewer to the next step: where to play, download, purchase or learn more. If you are on Steam Greenlight, you can also include the Greenlight URL here too.

Press Distribution Services

One of the easier ways to get information out there about your game is to use a press distribution service. Generally, for a fee, these services will target your release to a number of different industry press contacts.

GamesPress

Website: http://www.gamespress.com

One exception to the fee-paying rule is the wonderful GamesPress.

What They Say

"Games Press is the definitive one-stop PR resource for the games industry. The site is updated daily with press releases and artwork from publishers, developers, distributors and PR agencies, and we send out an email digest of new material each day. If you work in games PR it's the most effective way to put press releases, product information and assets at the media's fingertips."

Who Uses Games Press?

Games Press is used daily by over 50,000 registered users from all areas of the games industry, including:

► Specialist games magazines
► Lifestyle magazines
► National and local newspapers
► TV and radio
► Online media
► Fan sites
► All major UK high street and online retailers

So what else is out there? The following list includes the fee-charging distribution services, and details of their fees:

GameRelease.net

Website: http://www.gamerelease.net

GameRelease.net is a service for indie game studios to deliver press releases to the game journalists. Subscribe for free to receive email announcements about new indie games.

What They Say

"Start distributing your press releases using the indie licence. The indie licence is for small studios that want to promote their game using email and Twitter announcements. No, there's no licence for big studios. The indie licence costs $30 per two releases.

Indie licence grants you access to the members-only PR service and to the members-only game developers community. You may distribute your indie game press releases via the service. You will get to distribute two press releases and when you need more, you may simply purchase additional quota."

prMac

Website: http://prmac.com

What They Say

"prMac enhances the visibility of your press communications in the Apple universe, offering OS X and iOS related news media distribution services.

When you submit your Press Release for Extended Distribution, you can feel confident that it will be seen by those who have the ability to put your story in the media spotlight. With same day distribution, RSS/XML integration, and social media aggregation, prMac makes global Extended Distribution of all your Press Releases easy and affordable."

Most of the multipurpose app review sites repost prMac.com press releases, so it is a very useful resource for games on Apple platforms. There is a free option or the enhanced Extended Distribution, which includes:

► Listing on prMac.com Section Page
► Listing on prMac.com Home Page
► Subscribed User Email
► RSS/XML Inclusion
► Searching
► Next Day Distribution
► Improved Placement
► Ping RSS Aggregators
► Social Media Aggregation
► News Agency Email

SoftPress Release

Website: http://www.softpressrelease.com

SoftPress will develop and implement a comprehensive PR campaign to promote your game. A SoftPress promotion for an App or Game for Apple iOS, Android and Windows Phone apparently includes:

► Description writing for App Store or Google Play
► Writing quality press release text
► Press release distribution in specialized publications
► Review request distribution (English-language sites)

From the look of things, this could potentially get quite expensive very quickly.

Game Press Release Distribution Service at Mitorah Games

Website: http://www.mitorahgames.com/Submit-Game-Press-Release.html

What They Say

"Use the service to submit your game press release to over top 150+ computer games publications. All of the contacts have a strong online presence. Most are game news and reviews sites. Some are gaming magazine sites etc.

This is the most valuable way to market your game. Low cost, huge results. As a result, your game is likely to get many important sales bringing reviews and your website traffic and Google Page Rank will definitely get a major boost."

I am not entirely sure how successful a Mitorah release can be, and I don't really like their site wording. I would definitely suggest you ask them for a case study or two before you take the plunge.

Indie budget pricing:
▶ Game press release distribution for $59.95.
▶ Game press release distribution and co-writing for $99.95.

Tier One Services

The next level up, both in the number of contacts you can reach and the significantly higher costs, are the tier one services. These can be several hundred dollars per release, but the coverage can be very comprehensive. Probably not a viable choice for indie studios, but I will include them here for completion.

The tier one distribution companies are:
▶ http://www.businesswire.com/portal/site/home
▶ http://www.prnewswire.com
▶ https://globenewswire.com
▶ http://www.prweb.com

distribute()

The creators of presskit() are working on a new online press distribution service, called distribute(). Currently it is in the final stages of development, released to a small group of indie developers with an imminent wider launch planned.

What They Say

"distribute() is modelled to save you valuable development hours you'd otherwise have to spend on distributing builds and maintaining press lists. Simply send out a distribute() link for your game to your press contacts, and distribute() will organise all required information into a neatly organised list the system manages and maintains for you.

distribute() will handle the distribution of Steam-codes, iTunes promo codes, Humble links, PSN codes, Xbox redeem codes or any other token. It will also feature a verified press contacts service, to help you avoid fake requests from video content creators or people pretending to be from larger websites or YouTube personalities."

It certainly sounds like a service that could be a huge help to indie developers everywhere, and it is promised that it will be free to use for small studios. At the time of writing the wider launch date is unknown, but you can keep up-to-date with progress by signing up to the newsletter via the website: http://dodistribute.com.

Who Should You Contact?

The following sites are pro indie developers/indie games, so are a good place to start. This is only the tip of the iceberg though, for each platform you release on you will need to put together a dedicated list of sites and contacts. Be thorough and maintain something like an Excel spreadsheet where you can add notes next to each entry, so you always know whom you have contacted, when and what the outcome was.

Rock, Paper, Shotgun

Website: http://www.rockpapershotgun.com

A PC-only site, and one of the biggest around. They cover a lot of indie titles and appear to be a fairly approachable bunch.

Indie Games

Website: http://indiegames.com/index.html

Nothing but indie, a good place to target with your indie game. The site is packed with indie news, features and interviews, so what are you waiting for?

TIGSource

Website: http://www.tigsource.com

Probably the most indie of all indie games sites on the internet. There is also an excellent forum when you can discuss the various aspect of development with fellow indies.

Indie Game Magazine

Website: http://www.indiegamemag.com

You need to submit a game, demo or beta for inclusion and let them know if you are looking for a review or preview. There is no guarantee of inclusion, but it is a good place to be featured, as their readership is fairly large.

Pixel Prospector

Website: http://www.pixelprospector.com

Best 'About' description ever: "Pixel Prospector offers info about game development and is maintained by a guy who was born in the '80s."

The Indie Mine

Website: http://theindiemine.com

The Indie Mine was started in July 2011 out of a desire to shed light on unheralded or undervalued topics in the world of entertainment.

Insider Indie Q&A

1. What is the name of your studio?

Rie Studios Ltd

Logo and "RIE STUDIOS" © 2014 RIE STUDIOS LTD, all Rights reserved. Used with permission.

2. *What year was your studio founded and what are the names of the founders?*

2009, founded by Jay M Bedeau

Key team includes Tarik Bensaria (3D Artist), Aaron Thearle (Senior Programmer) and myself, Jay (Texture Artist & Illustrator).

3. *What are the studio's key game titles?*

Komodo Crunchtme®, Komodo Crunchtime® Ultimate Superstars

4. *Do you have your own in-house engine or use a third party system? If third party, which one do you use?*

We use Unity3D Professional.

5. *Which platforms do you release on now / plan to release on?*

Our upcoming releases are for iOS, Android and Facebook with PC and PlayStation Vita thereafter.

6. *Which is your most successful platform so far?*

Android

7. *What are the development tools you use most (i.e. 2D, 3D software, audio tools etc.)?*

Adobe Creative Suite

8. *What advice would you give to a new studio?*

Never over-inflate your self-perception; be humble, understand your weaknesses and be constructively critical. Review your project, listen to all members of the team and always get a second opinion from an industry source or your consumers.

Take your time. When your game is ready, it'll speak for itself. Plan your resources—especially time—obsessively. Understand your role as a developer exists in a symbiotic relationship with the health of the business. Business issues must be addressed (i.e. cash flow problems will always negatively impact your projects). Partner with other companies where possible. Think about who could get a vested interest in your product, and who can help bring your games to market. Remember, life gets in the way and that affects team morale.

9. *What marketing resources do you use?*

Extensive use of social media, specifically Twitter and Tumblr, lots of networking at events and now-and-then writing insights on blogs like Gamasutra. We also try to engage in CSR activities like teaching children and campaigning for rights of underrepresented players in gaming. Also, UKIE, UKIE, UKIE! They have been our strongest element in raising our profile. Again, I would strongly advocate becoming a member of organisations like UKIE or their overseas equivalents.

10. *What are your favourite indie games sites?*

For games that would be Steam, for news that would be IndieGameMag.com

11. *Any mistakes/hiccups you have made so far, something you would advise a new studio to avoid?*

Our biggest regret would be the lack of confidence we had within ourselves in terms of seeing things through without the assistance of others. Despite the hype that often surrounds gaming about funds and support, the reality is that going alone for as long as we could would have been the best thing we could have done as a studio. Despite exhaustive efforts, finance/investment remains difficult to access and we were founded just before indie became as huge as it is today. Indies are still looked down upon as hugely risky ventures. Finding the balance between allocating funds to the business' operating costs versus the current project is one that I feel you learn best from your mistakes. I can now see, in hindsight, being passionately artistic, we had often spent far too much on the project and had neglected things like our living expenses and our ability to live comfortably.

YouTubers Are the New Games Press

The gaming press has changed such a lot recently, and it stands to reason that indie studios should look for less traditional means to promote their games. YouTubers can have a big positive impact on your game promotion, with their audiences often much more receptive to indie game titles.

At this point, I'd like to point you in the direction of the fantastic Pixel Prospector/VideoGameCaster website. This site is the best thing on the internet for indie game developers. Featuring pages and pages of 'Big Lists,' which provide links to anything and everything indie game development related.

One such list is their YouTuber database, which is kept updated regularly and is now hosted on its own unique site:
▶ http://videogamecaster.com/big-list-of-youtubers

When you have a playable demo and are Early Access or Beta ready, start contacting the various YouTubers listed above. You can sort the list according to the interests of the YouTubers, such as Platformer, Arcade,

Shooter, Fighting, First Person Shooter, Horror, RPG, Adventure, Strategy, Simulation, Racing and more. If you can get covered by even one or two of these guys, you could see a boost in interest for your game. Get covered by one of the larger ones, and your game will hit the fast track!

One high profile indie example is 'Thomas Was Alone.' The developer has gone on record many times to say that the success of the title was helped by 'Let's Play' YouTube videos from Dan Hardcastle (aka Nerd Cubed). Apparently, the videos prompted a huge surge in popularity for the game.

Bear in mind, as with all media, most will likely not respond. Never be impatient or rude, but it can be a good idea to follow-up on initial communications a week or so later. One point to note, and this is the case with other online and print press, Kickstarter games are becoming less and less interesting to these guys. You could well have a very hard time trying to convince them to cover a Kickstarter demo, so it could be best to approach the coverage from another angle rather than specifying that it is a Kickstarter game.

As ever with any PR, timing is critical. You need to contact YouTubers before the game is out, give them access to preview/Beta builds. Leave it too late and it becomes very difficult to convince them to play your game, because there are always new games coming out. The launch window is everything. A good approach can be to send your game out a few weeks in advance of launch, and tell them that they can play whenever they want.

Try to avoid copyright music tracks, otherwise you will fall foul of YouTube's rules (see Monetization Worries below). What this means is that money would need to go to the composer of the song(s), rather than the YouTube creator. Naturally, the YouTuber will not want to be in that situation, so will most likely not cover the game (unless it is a major release).

You also need to consider that YouTubers often select to play games that are already popular, so using traditional online press can be very important to getting the attention of YouTubers in the first place. As such, make sure you don't neglect the more traditional games press coverage; you should see YouTubers as one segment of a larger press strategy.

Monetization Worries

In early December 2013, a change in YouTube's ContentID policy caused many existing Let's Play and other video game–related material to be blocked. This can still cause a few headaches, so make it nice and easy for everyone and create a valid monetization permission form for video content. Once again, the excellent guys at Vlambeer are here to help!

Simply fill in the details on their monetization form generator website here: http://vlambeer.com/toolkit/monetize-generator and all the necessary forms will be instantly generated for you.

Let's Play

A Let's Play (often abbreviated to "LP") is a recorded video documenting a play through of a video game, usually including commentary by the gamer. Let's Play videos focus on the individual's subjective experience with the game, often with humorous commentary. Many Let's Play videos also act as critical reviews of the game.

The biggest YouTubers, such as Felix Kjellberg (known by his online handle PewDiePie), have enormous reach. PewDiePie Let's Play videos reach over 27 million subscribers! Other major names include Rooster Teeth, The Yogscast, Smosh Games, Game Grumps, NerdCubed, TotalBiscuit, Northernlion and Machinima.com.

Howard Tsao, developer of Guns of Icarus Online had this to say on the subject, "Along the way, we realized how powerful these videos and YouTube casters are in getting the word out, especially for indie developers like us. For instance, one YouTube video had incredibly generated over $35K in sales for us on its first day of going live. The players who got the game through videos of casters such as TotalBiscuit, Jesse Cox or Yogscast were generally enthusiastic and engaged."

Borut Pfeifer of Skulls of the Shogun studio 17-BIT backs this up, saying, "Most indie game success stories on PC in the last year or two have had predominant YouTube coverage," he comments. "With Skulls we definitely sought people out and sent out hundreds of review codes to YouTubers, which is a lot more time consuming than regular press because they don't have consistent contact info."

A major Russian YouTuber, eligorko, covered the game, along with other smaller Russian YouTubers. Pfeifer believes this coverage helped to elevate Skulls of the Shogun to the second biggest seller in Russia for units sold.

Dan Pierce, UK developer of 10 Second Ninja backs this up, "As far as I've seen, we haven't had a significant spike from written press, but we have seen spikes from YouTube," he states. "Specifically, getting covered by Total Biscuit gave us a sales spike that roughly mirrored the game being on sale for a week. Getting covered by Dan NerdCubed brought in a bump of about half that, despite his video having roughly 100k more views."

Twitch

Twitch is a slightly different approach to YouTube, in that it is a live game-streaming service—where players and developers can live-stream game footage. More recently, developers have started using Twitch to broadcast live 'development' videos, showing the WIP development process. Interestingly, Twitch is now owned by Google, who also own YouTube—so there will be ever tighter integration between the two services.

Vlambeer were one of the first to use Twitch to broadcast footage of their game, Nuclear Throne, during development. This has now become quite a popular approach, with many developers following suit and broadcasting footage of themselves implementing features, creating artwork, testing levels and so on.

It is a good approach to building up a community from the very beginning of development, and really helps the developer to engage with their followers in a very hands-on way.

You can also add Twitch streaming directly to your game, with several game engines supporting this feature via plugins, to allow swift implementation. With in-built Twitch streaming, anyone playing your game can broadcast directly to Twitch from within the game.

Alternately, there are several applications out there, which can stream live to Twitch. These include:

Open Broadcaster Software
Website: http://obsproject.com

Open Broadcaster Software is free and open source software for video recording and live streaming. Key features include encoding using H264 (× 264) and AAC, live RTMP streaming to Twitch, YouTube, DailyMotion, Hitbox and more, file output to MP4 or FLV and Windows 8 high speed monitor capture support.

XSplit Gamecaster
Website: http://www.xsplit.com/products/gamecaster

Gamecaster is apparently the world's easiest and most versatile game streaming application. It has some great power features like built-in annotation for live onscreen drawing and chroma key green screen game face projection (should you wish to show off your ugly mug!). The downside is that it isn't free—with a premium commercial licence costing $24.95 for three months.

FFsplit
Website: http://www.ffsplit.com

FFsplit is a front-end solution that allows you to capture and composite videos. These videos can be encoded and streamed using Free Software, FFMPEG.

Insider Indie Q&A

1. What is the name of your studio?

Metanet Software Inc

© Metanet Software Inc.

2. What year was your studio founded and what are the names of the founders?

Founded in 2001, incorporated in 2004 by Mare Sheppard and Raigan Burns

3. What are the studio's key game titles?

N, N+ and N++

4. Do you have your own in-house engine or use a third party system? If third party, which one do you use?

We have our own engine. We like to have meticulous control over every aspect of a game.

5. Which platforms do you release on now / plan to release on?

PC, Mac, Linux, PS4, beyond that, who knows . . .

6. Which is your most successful platform so far?

PC/Mac/Linux, hands down

7. What are the development tools you use most (i.e. 2D, 3D software, audio tools etc.)?

Visual Studio, Flash, FlashDevelop and FlashBuilder, Illustrator, Photoshop, Goldwave and Audacity, Final Cut Pro

8. What advice would you give to a new studio?

Ultimately, you'll need patience, drive, determination and perseverance, and the knowledge that you will most likely fail repeatedly before being happy with anything you've done. Make sure the worth or value you see in your projects comes from you, and is not defined by outside sources like sales, fame, fans or press—you need to do what you do because you love it and you believe in it. If anyone else loves it too, that's a bonus, not the baseline.

Making games is gruelling and arduous, but also very rewarding and exciting. There's a long and difficult road ahead of you, and you need systems in place, strategies and friends to keep you motivated, creative and happy. When you make games because you believe in them and want to play more of them, and because you enjoy exploring creative ideas, then regardless of critical or commercial results, this can be the most enjoyable and satisfying work you could ever do. The payoff is immense: you get to watch your ideas come to life in surprising and dynamic ways, and you get to play something cool when you're done!

9. *What marketing resources do you use?*

We have a blog, a Twitter account and a Facebook. We make our own trailers and videos in-house and try to amp up the style in everything we release.

We rely heavily on word of mouth and grassroots marketing, and try to make sure our games are well defined and filled with personality, in the hopes that they really resonate with people, who then have something to talk about.

10. *What are your favourite indie games sites?*

Rock Paper Shotgun, TIGSource, itch.io, Twitter

11. *Any mistakes/hiccups you have made so far, something you would advise a new studio to avoid?*

Most first attempts are not our best attempts, so it's important to keep honing and refining ideas and their execution. It helps to surround yourself with other people who are interested in making games: sharing knowledge with experienced peers and providing feedback on each other's games is a hugely valuable resource that will help you iterate and improve your games over time.

Also, you need to be able to give your project, and yourself, the freedom to be something else. Flexibility in general is one of the most important skills you can have. You may become aware that something you're working on is more or less fun than expected, but feel that changing it is daunting since so much work/time/money has been spent on it. For example, we initially wanted our game N to be a slow-paced stealth game, until we discovered how fun it was to run and jump around the level at top speed—a huge divergence from our plans. Having the courage to change gears on the fly and maximize or minimize new discoveries can lead to some wonderfully unconventional outcomes and potentially a better game overall.

Reviews and Press Coverage

Indie developers need to be more aggressive in their promotion. Don't be humble about your game, or your company; shout about how great your game is and the fantastic stuff you are developing! The press will sit up and take notice of the more confident and self-assured releases, as it is those that catch the eye. If you can't big-up your own game, then who else will?

Make life easier for journalists by sending them preview/review copies without having to be asked. Consider offering exclusive content to your preferred sites/publications.

Make sure you also target non-game-specific publications, particularly if your game appeals to a particular niche group (for example, a golfing game).

Follow-up on Reviews and Online Articles

Join in the comments, even on bad reviews. Be open and honest, and if you plan an update to the game, a review comments section is a good place to promote it. Get input from existing users or potential customers for future features and improvements.

At Super Icon we recently had a very successful update release for our original PlayStation Mobile version of Life of Pixel. A few of the early reviews from games sites and users highlighted some negative issues, including lack of music variety and some cheap deaths in certain levels. We decided to go with a major 1.1 patch and re-engage with those reviewers, such as Indie Game Chick, who were not at all keen on the game the first time around.

I went through and re-played each level, removing all of the unfair deaths. We commissioned a brand new soundtrack, fixed a few performance issues and added a whole new set of levels. The response from players and press alike was very positive, even earning Pixel an 'Indie Gamer Chick Seal of Approval'!

The end result was that we had a game we were very happy with, and we built up a community of really good people following Pixel.

Tools and Resources

Promoter

Website: http://www.promoterapp.com

What They Say

"Designed for independent developers and studios from the ground up. Automagically track new press mentions of your games and apps. Get email notifications for new mentions to keep you and your team in the loop. Calculate average scores based on all press reviews."

Promoter is well regarded by many indie studios, and it makes the job of tracking reviews much easier. There are three different price plans available:

▸ Free plan includes 1 user, 1 product, 5 awards, 20 reviews and 50 promo codes
▸ Solo plan 10 EUR/month or 75 EUR/year
▸ Studio plan 20 EUR/month or 150 EUR/year

Promoter helps you keep track of any and all press mentions. It also has a fair few other tricks up its sleeve, including:

▸ Automatically track new press mentions of your games and apps.
▸ Calculate average scores based on all press reviews.
▸ Browse a list of 800+ gaming and tech websites grouped by platform, sorted by Twitter followers.
▸ See at a glance who you contacted and if they wrote a review.
▸ See how many Steam keys or promo codes you have left and when they expire.
▸ Compile the best press quotes on a great-looking promo page.
▸ Get reminders for festival deadlines—never miss IGF, IndieCade or PAX 10 again.
▸ Keep track of your awards, nominations and exhibitions.

I really like Promoter; it seems to work very well. During my tests it successfully notified me of all mentions my game received.

Google Alert

Website: http://www.google.com/alerts

A free service that will send you an email notification when your game is mentioned on the internet. You enter and save a Google search and it will let you know when new items match your search criteria.

MailChimp

Website: http://mailchimp.com

A bulk email and newsletter management program. You can use MailChimp to create, send and track email newsletters.

Create signup forms that match your brand/site's look and feel, and send your subscribers product updates, event invitations, announcements or editorial content. Analytics are included so you can generate reports to improve your campaigns and learn more about your subscribers.

If you have fewer than 2,000 subscribers, you can send up to 12,000 emails per month absolutely free.

Sendy

Website: http://sendy.co

What They Say

"Sendy is a self-hosted email newsletter application that lets you send trackable emails via Amazon Simple Email Service (SES). This makes it possible for you to send authenticated bulk emails at an insanely low price without sacrificing deliverability."

Sendy is another bulk mail option, which can work out much cheaper than other services when dealing with large volumes of email. You pay a one-time $59 payment to use, and minimal additional payments of $1 per 10,000 emails.

YMLP

Website: http://www.ymlp.com

YMLP is another popular newsletter management program. It includes a built-in email newsletter builder, with 30 sample templates. No CC, no BCC, no 'undisclosed recipients'—everyone gets their own copy, and can't see who else is receiving the same email.

Interestingly they even have a quote from Cliff Harris of Positech Games on their site, which in my opinion makes YMLP a very good choice as I value Cliff's opinion on this sort of thing:

> YMLP takes all of the hassle out of keeping in touch with people who like my games. Their reporting is excellent and the online user-interface makes putting together a nicely formatted press release a piece of cake. I'd recommend them to anyone who wants their newsletter signups handled professionally.

CHAPTER 5
Marketing

Know Your Market

The games industry is a fantastically creative place to be, but for every game you create, make sure you have an audience or a community of fans in mind from the very beginning. Try not to get swept away by creating a passion project and forgetting to factor in your market.

There is a marketer called Seth Godin who came up with the concept of building your 'Tribe.' Essentially, this means that you need to find those people who like what you are doing and give them somewhere to gather so you can feed them information. Get the message across to your tribe, and in turn they will spread that word, leading to a solid, organic growth of your followers. In practice this is a hard thing to achieve!

First off, your game concept. Approach each game concept from a purely objective business perspective—who would buy the game, is there a demand right now for such a game, are other similar games successful and so on. Again, challenge your assumptions—just because you think a certain feature is great doesn't necessarily mean your audience will agree. Consider the appeal of your ideas from the perspective of your audience—can you break the concept down to a one-line description that will explain why it's special and why the player would want to play it?

It is essential from the very beginning that you work out who is going to be interested in your game, and how and where you can reach them.

What Are Your Unique Selling Points (USPs)?

The characteristics of a product that can be used in advertising to differentiate it from its competitors.

Players and press alike are looking for something that stands out about your game, something that makes it special and worth their time and investment. A strong USP, even if it is slightly niche orientated, can make the difference between players merely liking your game, or loving it. The proposition must be one that other similar games do not offer; it must be unique.

Start Your Marketing Early

You can improve your chances of a successful game by building up your audience long before you release. Reach out to your target audience, give them regular updates and get them excited about your game.

Too many game developers spend all of their time developing their game only to leave marketing to the very end. Naturally, developing a great game is the key task, but without a strong marketing push throughout development, you can easily find yourself with a great game that nobody knows about. If nobody knows about your game, it will not sell, no matter how great it is.

You should really start marketing your game at the very least two months before launch, and ideally try to build up interest from the very beginning with your followers, your tribe. You can't just make a game and expect it to be successful.

Add a mailing list sign-up to your website to capture user data, which you can then use to keep those followers updated on the game's development progress, latest screenshots, gameplay videos and so on.

There are many aspects of the game creation process that your followers may find interesting, such as:

- ▶ Tell your story. How did you come up with the game concept?
- ▶ Post pictures of the team working on the game.
- ▶ Provide technical details of the development—such as packages and techniques used.
- ▶ Show concept sketches and in-progress artwork.
- ▶ Create a dev blog where you discuss the ups and downs of your development progress so far.
- ▶ Live-stream development progress and milestones as you achieve them.
- ▶ Discuss the inspirations behind the game.
- ▶ Make offline videos of your development progress.

Insider Indie Q&A

1. *What is the name of your studio?*

Puppygames

Puppygames and the Puppygames logo are trademarks of Shaven Puppy Ltd.

2. *What year was your studio founded and what are the names of the founders?*

Founded 2001 by Caspian Prince and Chaz Willets

3. *What are the studio's key game titles?*

- ▶ Revenge of the Titans
- ▶ Ultratron
- ▶ Titan Attacks!
- ▶ Droid Assault

4. *Do you have your own in-house engine or use a third party system? If third party, which one do you use?*

In-house 'engine.' Well, it is hardly an engine, just a bunch of code.

5. *Which platforms do you release on now / plan to release on?*

Windows, Mac and Linux, both direct sales and via Steam. We'll be fully compliant with Steam Big Picture mode soon, and hopefully we'll look good on the forthcoming Steambox. We'll be on PlayStation too in the not too distant future (PS3, 4, PSP, Vita) and Xbox360 via XBLIG.

6. *Which is your most successful platform so far?*

Steam for Windows

7. *What are the development tools you use most (i.e. 2D, 3D software, audio tools etc.)?*

Java, Eclipse, Adobe Photoshop, FruityLoops, Sony Vegas Pro

8. *What advice would you give to a new studio?*

Don't do it! It's a mug's game. And if that puts you off . . . maybe you really shouldn't be doing it.

9. *What marketing resources do you use?*

Our giant mailing list (nearly 80k subs), gamespress.com, ProjectWonderful. com. We've got a tiny presence on Facebook and Twitter (@puppygames) which we should try to grow one of these days.

10. *What are your favourite indie games sites?*

RockPaperShotgun and Indiegames.com equally.

11. *Any mistakes/hiccups you have made so far, something you would advise a new studio to avoid?*

Avoid making games that anyone else is making if you want to get noticed. I'd also generally advise avoiding the arcade game segment as we've not really done very well out of it. And finally, stay away from hi-tech. It's a time and money sink and as if that weren't bad enough, it shrinks your target market and finally and most damnably, it gives you so much scope for content, design and ideas that you'll end up just being a mess instead of focusing.

Marketing Checklist

I'll begin with a checklist of typical marketing activities you should begin immediately. Reach out to build up an audience, and make sure you keep up with these activities throughout development and after release.

Press Releases

Try to issue releases regularly; the goal is to keep both your company and games current. Make sure you include your promo trailer video link near the top of your game specific releases.

Typical events to mark with a press release include:
▶ Newly released game
▶ Interesting team member story
▶ Second game in a series in development
▶ Sales/download milestone reached or particular success earned
▶ Company milestone or achievement reached

YouTube

Create a YouTube account—upload your development diaries, WIP videos and promo videos in HD. Try to post videos regularly, and keep your channel current with the latest progress on your game's development. Aim to release a new video every week, to build traction with your YouTube followers.

Always try to use a custom thumbnail to go with your videos; you will need to verify your account before you can do this, but it really does make your videos look better so it is definitely worth doing.

Make sure you complete the 'About' section on your profile, and include all relevant company and game website links and social media links. Also associate your company website with your YouTube channel—you can access this via the 'Advance' menu.

The golden rule, as with any social media is to make sure you respond to any comments as they come in—don't leave your viewers waiting!

Twitter

Create a Twitter account. Typically this is an account that covers your entire company activities and all of your games, but you can also create a game-specific Twitter account. Make sure you fill out the Twitter Bio box—and try for a conversational tone, perhaps including your real name. Try not to be formal on Twitter.

Try to engage with your Twitter followers as much as possible, you will usually find them to be a good bunch. Remember they are following you because they want to hear what you have to say. Post regular tweets about your game's progress and ask for feedback and suggestions—start conversations about your game. Chat about things that interest you, don't be afraid to discuss non-work topics.

That said, aim for quality not quantity and don't post too many tweets—more than two or three tweets in an hour is known to decrease engagement.

Also consider that Twitter feeds are very dynamic and fast-moving. If you have important tweets, repost them multiple times at different times of the day/different days. Do make sure you reword them slightly each time you repost them though! If you write a lot of evergreen—content that is always relevant regardless of age—use a service such as Buffer to schedule and post tweets linking to the content, even when you are not around.

Always aim to split your tweets between your own news and developments, retweets of content you find interesting and replies to other interesting tweets. You can even adopt the 80/20 rule whereby you post non-promotional content 80% of the time, with the other 20% reserved for promoting your games and studio. Also, make sure you show appreciation for other tweets you like by marking them as favourites—you can build up a lot of goodwill by doing this.

Also try to use images where you can; tweets which include images are far more likely to be retweeted than plain text tweets.

Be sure to use #hashtags where appropriate (but don't go mad!). Hashtags can really help get a tweet seen by a much wider audience. A few examples to try are #screenshotsaturday, #indiedev, #indiegame. To help keep a watch on popular hashtags, check out these rather useful sites:
- ▶ Twitter Search (https://twitter.com/search-home)
- ▶ Hashtags (http://www.hashtags.org)
- ▶ What the Trend (http://whatthetrend.com)

Find out how influential you are by checking your Klout score (http://klout.com/home). The lower the score, the more often you need to tweet to increase the chances of retweets, replies and favourites. The goal is to expand your community of followers.

Make sure you include your Twitter contact details on all press releases, game menus and anywhere else you can. Add Twitter buttons to your website to allow your visitors to share content and connect with you on Twitter.

If you have a tweet that you would like to reach more people with, you can ask your followers to Retweet it (RT for short). Don't do this with every post though!

Another good approach to using Twitter to promote your game is to build functionality within your game. The game can then tweet to the player's Twitter feed once they reach certain game milestones. This could include sharing high scores or posting achievement awards earned in the game.

Searching Hashtags and Keywords

Another good use of Twitter is to search for hashtags and keywords that relate to your game or your studio. It is very likely that you will find other Twitter users discussing the genre, and from there, you can follow them, connect with them and let them know that you have a game they may well like.

Facebook

Create a Facebook 'page' rather than a personal profile account, and aim to post regularly with at least two or three new posts per week as a minimum. Make sure that you fill in as much of your studio's information as you can, so that visitors to your Facebook page can find out all they need to know about your studio without leaving the page.

You can also post screenshots, artwork and videos onto your Facebook page. Another useful feature I like to use are polls, which can be a great way to engage with your followers and get their opinion on certain game features.

When you have an important post, pin it to the top of your Facebook page (you can only do this for one post). All subsequent status updates will be listed below the pinned post. You should also make use of Timeline milestones, i.e. important milestones in your business past and present. These help to flesh out the history of your studio and provide visitors with an insight into your growth and development so far. You can also promote upcoming milestones before you reach them—perhaps in conjunction with competitions and giveaways.

You can also set up a Facebook page for each of your games, and invite any Facebook friends you already have to become fans of your new game page.

As with Twitter, include your Facebook contact details anywhere you can. You also have a number of other tools available for adding Facebook to your website, including:

Like Button
The Like button lets anyone share pages from your site back to their Facebook profile with one click.

Comments
The Comments box lets people comment on content on your website using their Facebook profile and show this activity to their friends in their own news feed.

Follow Button
The Follow button allows a visitor to quickly follow your Facebook page.

Twitter Link
Links Facebook to your Twitter account, so posts on Facebook will show up on your Twitter feed.

As discussed in the Twitter section above, it can really help raise awareness of your game to integrate social networks such as Facebook directly within your game. This could include sharing high scores or posting achievement awards earned in the game onto the player's Facebook page.

Tumblr

Tumblr is a micro-blogging social networking site, allowing users to post multimedia and other content to a short-form blog. You can design your Tumblr blog to closely match your studio branding and website, and it can be a great way to post newsbytes, screenshot and video updates, promo art, and so on. Keep it casual in tone, conversational rather than corporate speak.

Tumblr posts have more of a lifespan than Twitter and Facebook updates, so posts won't get lost so quickly. A nice feature of Tumblr is that when a visitor comments on your post, they have to repost it on their page, which can give your post a new lease of life.

Company Website

Create a website with interesting content such as development diaries, a regularly updated blog, game pages, contact information and any job listings. While certain sections of the website will need to be professional and corporate, you should also consider being more personal: discuss your current game development process, the background to starting your studio, the ups and downs, the tools and resources you use to develop games and so on.

Visitors are really interested in learning about how development works, the tools and technology you use, mistakes you've made that others can learn from and so on.

You need to be prepared to put a lot of time and effort into building up a community of followers. Aim for at least a weekly blog post and share as much insight as you can—put your game out there and be prepared to take criticism. It can take months to start building a list of followers, and you have to engage as much as possible. Keep up with any comments your readers make. Each blog entry also needs to include easily accessible social media widgets, so that any visitor who likes the post can easily pass it on to their followers.

Also make sure that every time you publish a new blog post you also post a link to the post on your other social media sites, such as Twitter, Facebook, Reddit. People don't tend to visit company websites on a regular basis, and are far more likely to notice a tweet or a Facebook post about the entry, and then go visit your site.

Product Website

It is a good idea to create a dedicated website for each of your games, either a single page as part of your company website or go the whole hog and create a dedicated game site with a game-specific URL, such as 'yourgame.com.' Be sure to include your description and features, screenshots and videos. List positive review quotes and scores near the top of the page.

A product website will be very similar in scope and content to a landing page or product description page, although you can include quite a bit more information, such as dedicated development progress blog posts.

Keep it current and up-to-date with any game updates and don't forget to include links to your Twitter, Facebook and other social media accounts.

Ensure you have a customer service section, reply form or email link on your website, so that customers can easily report issues or provide feedback.

Your game website should try to convince a potential customer to buy, so make sure you include prominent Buy Now 'Call-to-Action' buttons. Include a button for each store where your game is available to purchase.

Insider Indie Q&A

1. What is the name of your studio?

Four Door Lemon

2. What year was your studio founded and what are the names of the founders?

2005, Simon Barratt and Tim Wharton (left in 2008)

3. *What are the studio's key game titles?*

   Table Football (Vita), Table Mini Golf (Vita), Table Ice Hockey (Vita), Munch's Oddysee HD (PS3/Vita), Joe Danger 1 + 2 (Vita)

   Our main project right now is our own IP for release in 2014.

4. *Do you have your own in-house engine or use a third party system? If third party, which one do you use?*

   We have always use our own in-house engine for the majority of the technology in our games for both ourselves and clients. It covers a large variety of platforms and we're just finishing up the second iteration of it updated to target next-gen.

5. *Which platforms do you release on now / plan to release on?*

   We have always regarded ourselves as platform agnostic, focusing on the game and where the fans of it (hopefully!) are rather than the other way around. Our main project is likely digital downloadable on PC and console initially, with iOS and Android to follow.

6. *Which is your most successful platform so far?*

   In terms of our own titles, the iPhone with QuizQuizQuiz was the most successful with #1 across Europe on the App Store in 2009. With partners we coded Puzzler Collection on Nintendo DS which sold very well. For the most part we've worked on PlayStation platforms, however, and always really enjoy working with Sony be it work-for-hire or as a third-party developer/ publisher.

7. *What are the development tools you use most (i.e. 2D, 3D software, audio tools etc.)?*

   Our artists use 3D Studio Max, MotionBuilder, zBrush, Photoshop for the most part, though there are continuing temptations to switch to Maya!

   Code-wise, we're mainly based in Visual Studio for all platforms now though do use our own build configuration tools to help simplify some of our project setup.

8. *What advice would you give to a new studio?*

   Stay as nimble as you can for as long as you can, this means keeping overheads low, opting for working with contractors or business partners rather than employees. This will enable you to adjust quickly as you establish yourselves and put in the structure you need to grow.

9. *What marketing resources do you use?*

   We manage all of our marketing for our projects in-house currently and are currently hiring a PR/community person full time to help with our new project being announced and establishing the community around it. In the past, we've worked with external marketing teams for our work-for-hire projects and so have learnt a lot from them that we hope to apply. This is an area I've spent a lot of time talking to people about and understanding what we need to do to successfully market our games in the future; other people have correctly flagged this area as the hardest for developers to get right for many years now.

10. *What are your favourite indie games sites?*

I read a LOT of games sites regularly that cover mainstream and indie games—Rock Paper Shotgun, Indie Statik, Eurogamer, VG247, IndieGames.com, Guardian Blog, Pocket Gamer, Average Gamer to name a few!

11. *Any mistakes/hiccups you have made so far, something you would advise a new studio to avoid?*

We've made many mistakes!

Rather than a specific one to avoid I'd suggest creating a really good plan for how you regularly step back, evaluate how you're doing/identify issues and then ask yourself and the team 'Why?' over and over to get to the bottom of what the cause and therefore possible resolutions are.

User Ratings

Customer ratings and reviews can greatly influence sales of a game. Unfortunately, people often only provide a review when they have something negative to say, to vent about your game. A good way to try to increase positive reviews is to actually ask players to provide a rating, usually at a time when they are likely to be in a positive frame of mind toward your game. As such, try to time this with positive gameplay milestones or achievements, for example:

▶ After completing a level
▶ After earning a good high score
▶ After unlocking a key game event or reward
▶ After several days of play—if they haven't deleted it yet then they may well be enjoying the game

Good user reviews can really help to boost sales, so take the time to get this right.

RSS Feeds

RSS feeds are a great way to allow site visitors to easily keep track of your studio news and updates. Michael Rose, an editor at IndieGames.com, explains this from a journalist's perspective: "It's always a very good idea to have a working website available for viewing," he says. "The best kind of development sites are the ones which have separate pages for each different project, along with a blog which I can subscribe to the RSS feed of! That way I can check out an indie's games and keep up-to-date with all the latest from them via their blog."

Google's FeedBurner service (www.feedburner.com) is a great tool to use to expand your RSS functionality. Services include traffic analysis and automatic social media links within your feed. RSS subscribers can then share individual posts on Digg, Delicious, Facebook and more.

FeedBurner will also automatically send ping notifications to feed aggregators and search engines when you post a new blog entry.

ModDB/IndieDB

Websites: http://www.moddb.com and http://www.indiedb.com

ModDB and IndieDB can be a good way to reach out and build pre-release interest in your game. It is really easy to get started; you just need to add your company details and logos, and then a listing for each game. They are also closely linked to Desura, so ultimately you can publish your game via these pages.

Make sure you keep your game pages updated frequently as this will increase the chances of a news item being featured on the front page. If one of your updates does get featured on the front page, you can expect a big increase in your ranking on the site, and a whole lot more visibility for a few days.

Keep up with any comments. It is a decent community and in the main, you'll get to chat with some good people.

There is also a widget you can add to your game website that will show your game's current Mod/IndieDB ranking, and allow visitors a quick way to click and view your game page on the sites.

Screenshot Saturday

Website: http://screenshotsaturday.com

Screenshot Saturday is a great way to get screenshots of your game out there throughout the development phase. You just tweet a screenshot with the #screenshotsaturday hashtag and it will be automatically posted on

ScreenshotSaturday.com. Indie Game Mag also post digests of Screenshot Saturday content, which can also help to increase interest in your game.

Slidely

Website: http://slidely.com

Every game developer has a ton of screenshots. It's what we do—the quickest and easiest way to show off a game. But instead of just sticking them on a web page, how about showing them a little love; add a cool music track and some nice transitions, and then share them. This is where Slidely comes in.

With Slidely you can create beautiful photo galleries, add music and share on the web and mobile. You can also create video galleries, presented as a slideshow.

Digg

Website: http://digg.com

You can post about your game, or include a link to an article or video on Digg. Your submission will be posted immediately into 'Upcoming Stories.' If readers like it they will Digg it, but be prepared to post several articles before you get one that really takes off and becomes popular.

Competitions and Free Giveaways

Running competitions and free giveaways is a great way of building goodwill with users and the press. It is a good idea to build a relationship with key publications, where you can offer them something exclusive, rather than just a generic promotion.

You can also use this to communicate directly with your Twitter/ Facebook followers, for example:

▶ **The next 10 people to follow you on Twitter will each get a free download code for your game!**

Crowd Funding Increases Visibility

Sites like Kickstarter.com and Indiegogo.com are not only great places to help fund your game; they are also an excellent way to increase exposure for your game.

Even a failed campaign will help get the eyes of hundreds of gamers onto your game, and all for free!

It really is a win-win scenario, just be prepared to work bloody hard during the duration of the campaign. I recently ran a Kickstarter campaign for our game 'Life of Pixel', and while it was unsuccessful, we still gathered a lot more Twitter and Facebook followers and made some really good contacts. All in all, it was a very positive experience.

Steam Greenlight

Website: http://steamcommunity.com/greenlight

Steam Greenlight can be a good way to increase exposure, although do be wary if your game is a casual game or mobile port as these tend not to be successful on Greenlight.

They say: "Steam Greenlight is a system that enlists the community's help in picking some of the new games to be released on Steam. Developers post information, screenshots and video for their game and seek a critical mass of community support in order to get selected for distribution. Steam Greenlight also helps developers get feedback from potential customers and start creating an active community around their game during the development process."

You will need to fill out the submission form and pay a one-time $100 submission fee. The ultimate aim of greenlighting is to get your game accepted for distribution on Steam, but even if you aren't selected you will still get extra exposure.

Your game needs to be at a near complete stage before you can submit to Greenlight, although there is also a Concepts section:

"This section is intended for items looking to gather feedback from the potential customers and begin building a community."

There is no submission fee for a concept.

Reddit

Reddit is a social news and entertainment website where registered users submit content in the form of either a link or a text ('self') post. Other users then vote the submission 'up' or 'down,' which is used to rank the post and determine its position on the site's pages and front page. Content entries are organized by areas of interest, called 'subreddits.' Of particular relevance to indie developers are these game-specific subreddits:

IndieGames (http://www.reddit.com/r/indiegames)
IndieGaming (http://www.reddit.com/r/IndieGaming)
These two subreddits cover various aspects of indie gaming and development: A good place to post trailers, game info and development blog entries.

Game Dev (http://www.reddit.com/r/gamedev)
Covering a variety of game development posts such as code, design, tech and art.

Make sure you post an article that is worth reading, rather than just cutting and pasting a press release. Be aware of your reddiquette—reddit users don't take kindly to spam: http://www.reddit.com/wiki/reddiquette.

Try to be an active member of the community, comment on other posts and make sure you use attention-grabbing headlines for your posts. It isn't easy though, and they can often be a funny bunch, banning posts that they believe fall foul of the rules—which include self-promotion!

Reddit has actually caused more than a few ripples for some developers, including a certain Matt Rix, who developed an iOS game called Trainyard. The link below explains the amazing story in full, but to summarise, he posted about his game on reddit, asking users to buy it so that he could top Angry Birds in the charts. Amazingly they did—and he actually did top Angry Birds in the charts! Inspiring stuff. http://www.reddit.com/r/iphone/comments/dq8pz/dear_reddit_with_your_help_my_iphone_game_can/

Conferences, Festival Contests and Game Jams

Websites:
http://www.igf.com
http://www.indiecade.com
http://www.unrealengine.com/msul
http://globalgamejam.org

The main competition at the Independent Games Festival is one of the best opportunities for an indie development studio to get noticed. Finalists are also offered Steam contracts by Valve for their games, so it is a fantastic opportunity. The press really do take notice of IGF finalists.

Other high profile competitions and festivals include IndieCade (International Festival of Indie Games) and Make Something Unreal.

The PromoterApp Calendar offers a great way to keep on top of all the upcoming game festivals and competitions, you can view here: http://www.promoterapp.com/calendar and also sign up for email alerts.

Game Conferences are an excellent networking opportunity, and many of the festivals are linked to the larger conferences. Once again, there is a great website service available to help you keep track of upcoming conferences, so head on over to Gameconfs to get a full list: http://www.gameconfs.com.

There are also many different Game Jams you can participate in, which can offer a good opportunity to raise your profile and meet other indie developers.

The Compohub website is a great way to find current and upcoming game jams. It keeps track of when game jams happen, and you can also submit your own jams—point your browser to: http://compohub.net.

Analytics

Analytics tools help you to track all of your publishing data across the various app stores, allowing you to use this data to describe, predict and improve your game's sales performance. There are many different analytics solutions out there, and in general, they enable you to track revenue, downloads, ratings, reviews and rankings. Analytics are only really available on the more open mobile platforms, such as iOS and Android, and to a lesser extent certain computer stores such as the Mac AppStore.

Unfortunately, traditional consoles don't really offer much in the way of analytics, with facts and figures often shrouded in platform-holder enforced secrecy. Hopefully this will improve in the future, although don't necessarily hold your breath!

App Annie

Website: http://www.appannie.com

Perhaps the most well known of the app analytics solutions, App Annie offers a wide range of services including analytics, store stats and charts, market insight reports and the very expensive App Annie Intelligence.

Intelligence sounds good, apparently allowing you to download revenue estimates for every app, publisher, category and country. Alas, you most likely won't be able to afford it, but the great news is that *SensorTower* offers similar functionality for free.

App Annie offers many of its other services for free, including analytics, store stats and insight reports. To access these you just need to register a free account and you're good to go. You can track your app data across iTunes, Google Play and Amazon.

Flurry

Website: http://www.flurry.com/flurry-analytics.html

Flurry Analytics is completely free, and allows you to track how users interact with your app, learn about your audience, monitor your advertising and more. You can also use the Flurry SDK to monitor crash reports for your apps.

Flurry Analytics is available for iOS, Android, Windows Phone, HTML5/Hybrid Apps/MobileWeb, BlackBerry and JavaME.

Swrve

Website: http://www.swrve.com

Apparently Swrve is dedicated to one thing only: building lasting, personalized relationships with your mobile app consumers. This equates to in-depth user analytics to allow you to target your marketing. Define target groups by any combination of criteria—including acquisition source, customer value and pretty much any aspect of user behaviour you want to track. Swrve provides details on item sales, total spend and ad revenues.

Apmetrix

Website: http://www.apmetrix.com

Apmetrix is a relatively new service founded by former video game publishing executives including Lee Jacobson, formerly of Midway Games. With an advisory board comprised of some big industry names such as Nolan Bushnell and Brian Fargo, this could potentially be a good solution for game developers.

Apmetrix provides a complete cloud-based analytics solution for game and app developers that communicates and rewards players based on their play, including:

- ► Real-time reports for all your game and app metrics and vendors
- ► Analyse player behaviours to gain insights to increase revenues
- ► View your ad revenue and acquisition campaigns to identify which ones provide the best lifetime value
- ► Use the analytics data to automatically send messages and rewards to players to increase monetization
- ► Access your data on the go using the iOS and Android app

Marketing Tools

There are several very useful internet marketing tools available that are either completely free to use, or offer their services for a low indie-friendly cost. I've included a selection of the most popular and well-respected tools below; these can really help to build an effective marketing campaign.

Buffer

Website: http://bufferapp.com

Buffer helps you spread the word about your indie game across multiple social media accounts at once. Quickly schedule content from anywhere on the web, collaborate with team members and analyze detailed statistics on how your posts perform. Write a series of posts at one time and choose which social profiles to send them to, and then Buffer will spread them out throughout the day or week so that you don't have to be at a computer all the time in order to have a social media presence.

In addition, Buffer shortens your links for you, and is able to provide more analytics than if you just post to Twitter or Facebook directly. As an example, Buffer can tell you exactly how many people clicked on each of your links.

Social Mention

Website: http://socialmention.com

Real-time social media search and analysis. Enter a search term, and Social Mention will return results based on the social media buzz for that term. This could be your game title, genre, studio name and so on.

You can monitor various channel types, including blogs, microblogs, bookmarks, images, videos or questions. You can then sort the results via time, date and source.

IceRocket

Website: http://www.icerocket.com

IceRocket allows you to search Blogs, Twitter and Facebook all from one page. Type a term into the search box, select the channel you want to search and then check the results. You can then filter the results by links, text or hashtags. IceRocket also displays an average posts-per-day count.

CrowdBooster

Website: http://crowdbooster.com

CrowdBooster is a thoroughly comprehensive, yet simple-to-use tool that will allow you to visually see how well your posts, tweets and so on are performing. It allows you to track the growth of your audience and see the benefits of long-term engagement or the effectiveness of a one-time social media campaign.

Check the number of retweets, replies, impressions, likes, comments and many more metrics, all customizable by date range, all in real-time so you can quickly adapt to your audience's reaction.

Do you want to find out who is your biggest fan? How about your most enthusiastic retweeter? Do you know who they are? Use Crowdbooster to find your biggest social advocates and show them how much you love them, too.

You can also schedule as many tweets and Facebook posts as you'd like, all at the most optimal time as calculated by Crowdbooster to maximize reach.

CrowdBooster isn't free, but the good news is that most indies will only need the basic plan, which covers 1 user, 1 Twitter user and 1 Facebook page and up to 50,000 fans + followers. This 'Bronze' plan is just $9 per month, so nice and affordable.

Marketing Grader

Website: http://marketing.grader.com

A free online tool that will analyse your site, social media presence and overall online influence. Your site is rated with a score out of 100, along with a checklist of actionable items to do to improve this. The areas covered include lead generation, SEO, social media and blogging.

Inbound Writer

Website: http://www.inboundwriter.com

A great tool to help you produce marketable blog content. Inbound Writer provides valuable feedback to make your posts more appealing to internet users based on various criteria and search results. This rather clever bit of software performs various tasks such as:

- Generating ideas on what to write about
- Predicting performance of your written content before you make the investment to write it
- Improving content quality in a consistent and scalable way
- Measuring results connecting content quality to traffic and engagement

It will also give you feedback on:

► The size of your audience for a given topic
► Who else is publishing content on that topic (your competition)
► The most productive terms you can use for that topic

HootSuite

Website: https://hootsuite.com

HootSuite is apparently the leading social media dashboard to manage and measure your social networks. Essentially this will allow you to manage your various social marketing activities from one program. I have used HootSuite a little, but I was surprised that it didn't include notification tracking for major social networks such as reddit, so that reduced its appeal to me.

Features include:

► Manage multiple social networks
► Schedule social messages and activities
► Analytics tools and customizable reports that will give you a complete and comprehensive picture of your participation in social spaces
► Track statistics such as the number of followers, lists, mentions and more

Google Analytics

Website: http://www.google.com/analytics

You can use Google Analytics to track how people find your site and which websites refer them. Thus you can quickly build up a profile of your most successful marketing methods. You can then take things a step further and analyse how visitors interact with your pages.

Google Analytics offers a lot of depth and can really help you to monitor how successfully your marketing campaign is progressing.

Klout

Website: http://klout.com/home

The Klout Score is a 1–100 number showing how influential you are in the world of social media. In determining the user score, Klout measures the size of a user's social media network and correlates the content created to measure how other users interact with that content.

Be warned—Klout can become an obsession, especially if you get beyond a score of 50 and start receiving Klout Perks. Rumor has it that if you get a Klout score above 90, you never need to buy anything ever again!

Klout offers a way to gauge how effective your social media efforts are, and identifies the most influential people in your network.

SurveyMonkey

Website: https://www.surveymonkey.com

Online surveys can be a great way to gather user feedback, and SurveyMonkey is one of the best. It offers a free plan, which includes the following features:

► 10 questions per survey
► 100 responses per survey
► Web-based survey tool
► Collect data via weblink, email, Facebook or embed on your site or blog

---

Insider Indie Q&A

1. *What is the name of your studio?*

Cellar Door Games

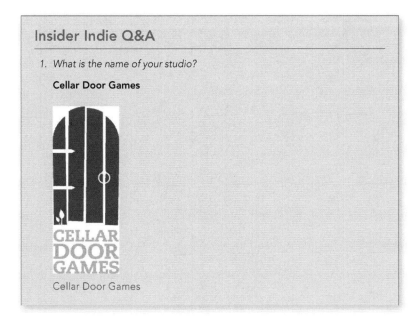

Cellar Door Games

2. *What year was your studio founded and what are the names of the founders?*

Founded: 2009

Founders: Kenny Lee and Teddy Lee

3. *What are the studio's key game titles?*

Rogue Legacy

Don't Shit Your Pants

4. *Do you have your own in-house engine or use a third party system? If third party, which one do you use?*

In-house engine

5. *Which platforms do you release on now / plan to release on?*

Currently released on PC, Mac, Linux, PS3, PS4, PSV.

Not sure where we plan to release future products. We're not that forward thinking.

6. *Which is your most successful platform so far?*

PC

7. *What are the development tools you use most (i.e. 2D, 3D software, audio tools etc.)?*

Photoshop, Visual Studios, Excel and Flash

8. *What advice would you give to a new studio?*

Make a small game first, but see it through. If you're only creating half-finished projects, you're not learning anything.

9. *What marketing resources do you use?*

We have no marketing power. We just send out hundreds and hundreds of emails. And we follow-up with as many people as we can.

10. *What are your favourite indie games sites?*

indiegames.com, I guess. We don't really go to indie exclusive game sites.

11. *Any mistakes/hiccups you have made so far, something you would advise a new studio to avoid?*

Don't ignore the business portion of your studio. It will bite you in the butt.

CHAPTER **6**

Advertising

Advertising is traditionally an area that many indies tend to ignore, primarily due to lack of funds. Over the past few weeks I have researched several different articles on advertising indie games, and the common observation across them all is that it isn't really worth advertising unless you can set aside a budget of at least $500.

Once you do launch your advertising campaign, make sure you check results on a daily basis. All advertisement sites include analytics tools, so make sure you use them. Check which sites perform best and suspend poorly performing sites/adverts. Never just leave a campaign to run itself, as you will see poor results and you will have wasted your investment.

There are several different ways you can advertise an indie game, which I will cover below. First off though, let's get to grips with the typical advertising types. There are three primary methods for online advertisement charging:

Cost per click, or CPC, is where you, the advertiser, pay the website owner when your ad is clicked. It is defined simply as "the amount spent to get an advertisement clicked."

Cost per impression, or CPM, refers to the model where you pay for every time an ad is displayed. Specifically, it is the cost to offer potential customers one opportunity to see the advertisement.

Cost per day, or CPD, serves ads on the basis of time. In cost per day, the advertiser pays a fixed cost per day an advertisement is displayed. Smaller sites may also offer a monthly cost to display an advertisement for a full month.

Each ad site will use one or more of those methods. I prefer cost per clicks (CPC), but there are not many places that do this so you will most likely be dealing with CPM or CPD methods.

Advertising Channels

I have compiled a list of the most popular and well-regarded advertising channels for indie games. Bear in mind this isn't an exhaustive list; there are other options out there that I haven't covered. These are the sites most commonly recommended by indie developers as being the most cost-effective and efficient ways to advertise an indie game.

Reddit

Website: http://www.reddit.com/ad_inq
Ad Model: Cost per impression

There are two types of ads you can run on reddit: 'frontpage' and 'targeted.' You specify the start and end date, between which you'd like your reddit promotion to run. Your promotion will start on the start date, and end at 12 a.m. on the end date.

Frontpage Advertisement
Your promotion will rotate on the reddit homepage ('reddit.com').

Targeted Advertisement
Your ad will show up in two sections:

1. Top spot on the subreddit being targeted. If there is more than one person (or more than one ad) targeted to that subreddit on the same day, your ad will rotate with those ads as well.
2. On the front page of a user who is logged in and subscribes to that subreddit. This will rotate with other ads that are targeted to other subreddits that user is subscribed to, along with front page ads.

You are charged a flat fee for every 1,000 impressions you want to receive. The reddit CPM rate is $0.75, so 75 cents per 1,000 times your ad gets 'delivered' (displayed to a redditor).

The minimum spend per campaign is $5.

Reddit advertising can be very effective because you can specifically target the gaming subreddits. As with any reddit activities make sure you understand the reddit audience first, which can vary for each subreddit. Present your game in a way that would appeal to them and always remember your reddiquette!

Project Wonderful

Website: https://www.projectwonderful.com
Ad Model: Cost per day

Project Wonderful offers a unique approach whereby you don't get charged for clicks or display, instead, just name your price for a day's worth of advertising; when you're the high bidder, your ad is displayed. You can alter or cancel your bids in real time, and even advertise for free (if your bid is at $0, and you're the high bidder, the ad is free).

As a result of this unique approach, Project Wonderful can make advertising accessible to indie studios on a budget.

BuySellAds

Website: http://buysellads.com
Ad Model: Varies depending on publisher

Access thousands of quality, pre-screened publishers with a wide variety of pricing options. It is very straightforward to use:

1. Browse or search the marketplace for ads you'd like to buy
2. Select your placements
3. Upload creative
4. Checkout

Once you have paid for your ad(s), your order will be submitted to each publisher and they will either approve or deny your ad within 24 hours.

You can then manage and optimize your campaign, see how your ads are performing, try different versions of creative with the A/B testing feature. Any placements that aren't working can be cancelled, and new ones booked.

iSocket

Website: http://www.isocket.com
Ad Model: Varies depending on publisher

iSocket used to be called BuyAds, and it looks very different now. I have included it here, but I don't have any recent information from indies on how well it now works for them since the brand change. In all honesty, it now looks rather daunting and expensive!

What They Say

"iSocket for Advertisers is an automated way to buy well-defined, guaranteed inventory directly from premium publishers. iSocket never blends inventory from multiple publishers or placements, so you always know exactly what you're buying. iSocket combines all the benefits of buying directly with the efficiency of programmatic."

Google Adwords

Website: http://www.google.com/adwords
Ad Model: Cost per click

One great feature of Google Adwords is that you pay only if people click on your ads and visit your website. I much prefer this approach to a CPM type method, as you can be certain you are actually getting traffic as a result of your ad.

Keyword Search Ads

You create ads and choose keywords, which are words or phrases related to your business. When people search on Google using one of your keywords, your ad may appear next to the search results.

The key to Google Adwords is to be very specific with where and how you advertise. First off, just select a few countries; if you have an English language game it is probably best to stick to the English language.

As an example, at Super Icon our PlayStation sales figures provide a useful insight into our highest selling markets, with our best numbers coming from:

- ▶ USA
- ▶ UK
- ▶ Germany

- ► France
- ► Canada
- ► Spain
- ► Netherlands
- ► Australia
- ► Belgium
- ► Italy

You can also select your target age range if you have one. The most important thing to remember with an Adwords campaign is don't just let Google choose where to place your ads, choose the sites to target yourself. Take charge of your campaign!

Also be aware that you can specify where not to target (i.e. if you have a PC game, you don't really want to target mobile users). You can also specify make and model of phones and tablets to target, so you can be very specific.

Try to keep things as simple as you can. Cliff Harris of Positech Games offers some great advice on his site (http://positech.co.uk/cliffsblog/2013/10/11/what-i-think-i-know-about-advertising-as-an-indie-game-developer/):

"I aim to get clicks for around $0.30 or less, depending on the game I'm promoting. Note that google has very strict rules about ad text. I got an ad banned for saying 'Mac', without Apples permission. If your display ads take a while to be approved, email and complain, then they get done."

Facebook

Website: https://www.facebook.com
Ad Model: Cost per impression

Every single indie blog I have seen that mentions Facebook ads says don't do it, they are a waste of time. So I shall take that advice and ignore standard Facebook ads.

A better option is to boost individual posts. I've done this a few times, and in general, it works well, promoting the post to the right sort of people who are most likely to be interested in your post.

Boosted posts last for three days and increase the reach of your post beyond your regular followers. To get the best results, wait a few hours before boosting a post, let it hit its natural reach first. Boost posts that drive engagement rather than just likes—such as a new game launch, with an included Call-to-Action. Don't forget to pin boosted posts to the top of your page for the duration of the promotion.

It is really easy to do, each post has a Boost post button, you select how much money you wish to pay, choose a payment option and click go. Your post will then be promoted until your budget runs out. You should also measure its success via the Facebook Insights and other analytics tools.

Banner Sizes

Ad specifications vary depending on how much you are spending, and the sites you target. Most ads use the IAB (Internet Advertising Bureau) display standards sizes. The most common sizes are:

300 × 250 pixel—MPU/Medium Rectangle
300 × 600 pixel—Half Page
728 × 90—Leaderboard
468 × 60—Banner
120 × 600—Skyscraper
160 × 600—Wide Skyscraper

A full list of typical banner sizes can be found here:
► http://en.wikipedia.org/wiki/Web_banner.

Insider Indie Q&A

1. *What is the name of your studio?*

New Star Games

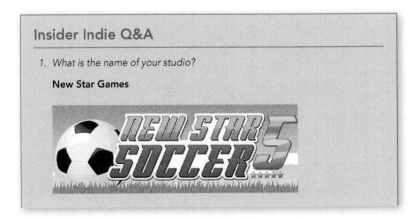

2. *What year was your studio founded and what are the names of the founders?*

   2006 Simon Read / Lucy Read

3. *What are the studio's key game titles?*

   ► New Star Soccer
   ► New Star GP
   ► Super Laser Racer

4. *Do you have your own in-house engine or use a third party system? If third party, which one do you use?*

   I use Monkey to code the game, which allows us to build easily on multiple platforms.

5. *Which platforms do you release on now / plan to release on?*

   iOS, Android, Flash, PC, Mac. The future may see titles on console but this is unconfirmed at the moment.

6. *Which is your most successful platform so far?*

   iOS by far.

7. *What are the development tools you use most (i.e. 2D, 3D software, audio tools etc.)?*

   Monkey, Paint Shop Pro, Sound Forge

8. *What advice would you give to a new studio?*

   Don't aim too high too soon. Start with small projects and scale up slowly.

9. *What marketing resources do you use?*

   None.

10. *What are your favourite indie games sites?*

    Indiegames.com

11. *Any mistakes/hiccups you have made so far, something you would advise a new studio to avoid?*

    I tried to make a 3D football game with a huge player database that was just far too ambitious for a one man studio. The game did launch but was beset with problems right from the start and drained my energy and enthusiasm over the subsequent years. I have since learnt that smaller, more focused titles are the way forward for me.

Mobile Advertising

On the flip side of the coin, indie developers can also earn money from adverts, in the form of ads in your own game. Mobile ads can be a good way to make money from free games (ad-supported games). There are many different ad services you can sign up with, and all are free to join.

Most ad networks allow you to turn ads on and off at will, so you can easily implement an In-App-Purchase (IAP) to turn off ads. Another approach, and one that is more consumer friendly, is to tie ad removal into your other IAPs. Tell users that making any sort of purchase in the game will remove ads forever. A $0.99 purchase is worth more to the developer than the player would generate in lifetime ads. Additionally, it boosts goodwill and increases the chances of them making a second purchase in the future.

One important point to note is that not all games are suited to in-game advertising. Games aimed at a younger audience are not really a good fit; parents will get annoyed and there are many new acts of legislation being introduced in different regions to protect children from such nastiness, so tread carefully here. Quite rightly so, I should add.

3D games are also not ideal, as onscreen adverts really destroy the illusion of an immersive 3D world. Casual games tend to be a much better fit for in-app advertising, with games such as Angry Birds Free showing how such ads can be integrated seamlessly.

Last, you should also consider cross promoting your other game titles within each game you release. You can also up-sell paid apps and in-app purchases from free versions of your games. Free game releases on larger stores like the App Store can potentially hit a much larger audience than paid apps, so this in turn can be used to promote other games you have published.

Ad Networks

Google Admob Ads

Website: https://www.google.com/ads/admob

Ads from Google advertisers are displayed in your app and users click on the ads they like. You earn money every time a user clicks on ads in your app. Admob is cross-platform, supporting iOS, Android and Windows 8.

Do you remember 'Flappy Bird' and the insane amount of ad revenue the creator earned from that game? Flappy used Admob ads, and it made him very happy!

Apple's iAd

Website: https://developer.apple.com/iad/resources

Apple's own ad system is very popular with iOS developers (naturally), and you earn 70% of the ad revenue generated.

Applovin

Website: https://www.applovin.com/developers

Applovin gets quite a few positive recommendations from indie developers, and from what I have seen of figures, the earnings were a little better than some ad networks. Applovin is available for Android and iOS.

Chartboost

Website: https://www.chartboost.com

Chartboost promises to increase your in-app purchase revenue and allow you to make changes in real-time with Chartboost Store, their backend service for mobile game developers. Chartboost is all about the cross promotion of games; you can advertise other developer's games, or even cross-promote your own titles.

RevMob

Website: http://www.revmobmobileadnetwork.com

RevMob is a Cost-Per-Install (CPI) network that offers the highest eCPM for game publishers. RevMob supports iOS, Android and Amazon.

Tapjoy

Website: https://www.tapjoy.com/homepage

Tapjoy allows you to make changes quickly and easily through the self-service Tapjoy dashboard. Adjust ad placements, customize

messages, segment your user base and more, all without updating
your code.

Upsight (Formerly Playhaven)

Website: http://www.upsight.com

Apparently, Upsight is one of the most flexible ad networks to manage,
offering a lot of control over the ads appearing in your game. You
can cross-promote other games, offer virtual rewards and make
announcements (for events such as app updates and holiday promos).

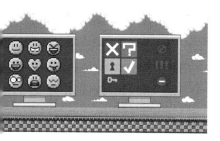

CHAPTER **7**
Websites, Forums and Source Control

Company Website

There are several different solutions out there for authoring websites, but for any site with lots of content and regular additions, in my opinion, there is only one choice and that is WordPress. It is an amazing solution, completely free and incredibly fully featured and adaptable.

Landing pages and game-specific sites are a different kettle of fish, and a more design-focused solution such as Adobe's *Muse* could be a better option.
Website: http://wordpress.org

What They Say
"WordPress is web software you can use to create a beautiful website or blog. We like to say that WordPress is both free and priceless at the same time."

I have used WordPress to create many different sites: company sites, game sites, campaign blogs and more. When combined with the numerous free plugins and site theme templates you can literally create any sort of site with just a few hours' work.

Theme Templates

One of the most amazingly useful features of WordPress development is the pre-built themes. With a single click these bad boys will completely change the design of your site and add all sorts of different functionality. In the past, web design like this would have cost many thousands; now you'll find amazing themes for less than $50, or often free.

If you can't already tell, I really do love WordPress!

WordPress Themes

There are several points you should look for when choosing a theme for your site. You need a theme that is easy to navigate, with a single click to take visitors to information on your games. Never make visitors hunt for content on your site; everything needs to be intuitive, cleanly designed and easy to navigate.

Make sure your site is optimized for search engines (Search Engine Optimization, SEO for short). You need to be able to edit the page's title, description and header tags and use perma-links for categories. A good place to start is to peruse the free *SEO Starter Guide* provided by Google:

▶ www.google.com/webmasters/docs/search-engine-optimization-starter-guide.pdf

Ensure the theme features built-in social media sharing buttons, in a prominent position. You can also expand on this with plugins, which will add social buttons to each blog post. Make it easy for visitors to share content from your site.

Other important site functionality includes a built-in newsletter subscription form, which encourages visitors to sign-up and receive updates about your games. This can be a great way to keep in touch with the followers who are most interested in your games and studio.

Last but by no means least, RSS functionality. This is an essential feature, allowing people to easily follow developments at your studio, and progress on your games, as and when they happen.

Let's take a look at some of the best places to find WordPress themes:

WooThemes
Website: http://www.woothemes.com

A nice variety of attractive and well-programmed themes, with an excellent framework common to all of their themes. I have used Woo many times, and their themes are rock solid and regularly updated to support current WordPress features.

ThemeZilla
Website: http://www.themezilla.com

ThemeZilla is similar to WooThemes, i.e. a small-ish range of premium WordPress themes and plugins. Apparently, over 30,000 customers use ThemeZilla themes to power their websites.

ThemeForest
Website: http://themeforest.net

Theme Forest offers a massive selection of themes, with many stunningly good examples of WordPress theme design. Be careful when you choose though, as some themes can be a little unreliable. Use the theme ratings as a guide when selecting a theme to buy.

Themes&Co
Website: http://www.themesandco.com

Customizr is a free and easily customized theme offering many of the standard features you can expect from a premium website template.

WP Eden
Website: http://wpeden.com

A varied selection of WordPress themes, WordPress plugins, tips and tutorials.

ThemeZee
Website: http://themezee.com/themes/

Clean, nicely designed freemium themes. Several additional Pro Themes, with more functionality, are available for an annual fee of $35—this includes access to all Pro themes on the site.

Colorlib
Website: http://colorlib.com/wp
Colorlib offer a few high quality, free and premium WordPress themes. I have used the Sparkling theme, and it is a really solid and easy to use theme.

WordPress Optimization

While WordPress is a very efficient platform, it can run wild on a server—especially with several plugins running. This can have a detrimental effect on your site in a number of ways:

► SEOs—although relevance is the primary SEO factor, website loading speed is also an important factor
► User experience—visitors to your site really do hate waiting for pages to load, it just looks unprofessional
► Google ranking—Google will rank slow loading sites lower in their search results

A good plugin to use to improve your WordPress SEO is the WordPress SEO plugin by Yoast.
Website: https://wordpress.org/plugins/wordpress-seo

What They Say
"This plugin is written from the ground up by Joost de Valk and his team at Yoast to improve your site's SEO on all needed aspects. While this WordPress SEO plugin goes the extra mile to take care of all the technical optimization, it first and foremost helps you write better content. WordPress SEO forces you to choose a focus keyword when you're writing your articles, and then makes sure you use that focus keyword everywhere."

If you are serious about SEO, this plugin is a great place to start. Just look at the stats—2989 five-star ratings on Wordpress.org—that is the highest rated plugin I've seen.

Web Caching Plugins

On a WordPress site it is important that content is retrieved from your database as swiftly as possible. The default WordPress settings can be a little slow, particularly for a larger site. Fortunately, there are several free Plugins available to help speed up your database interaction.

One point of note is that these plugins can make it so that changes and updates to your site aren't seen by users for a delayed period of time—five minutes to an hour. Just temporarily disable the plugins when updating/testing your site.

WP Super Cache

WP Super Cache is a static caching plugin for WordPress. It generates html files that are served directly by Apache without processing comparatively heavy PHP scripts. By using this plugin you will speed up your WordPress blog significantly.

Hyper Cache

Hyper Cache is a powerful cache system for WordPress websites. It is made for those users with low-resources hosting providers.

W3 Total Cache

W3 Total Cache is the most popular WordPress caching plugin. Thousands of WordPress sites such as yoast.com, css-tricks.com, mashable.com and smashingmagazine.com use this plugin. W3 can help increase website load speeds by up to ten times.

The following plugins work in conjunction with those above, to further speed-up a WordPress site:

WP Widget Cache

WP will cache the output of all of your blog widgets. Usually it will significantly reduce the SQL queries to your database and speed up your site. This is a good thing as Widgets can be one of the slowest features of a WordPress site.

Database Optimization

Ideally, you should regularly optimize your MySQL database to avoid a 'fragmentation' effect. WP-DBManager is the tool to use.

WP-DBManager manages your WordPress database allowing you to optimize, repair, back up and restore the database. You can also use it to delete backup databases, drop/empty tables and run selected queries. WP-DBManager supports automatic scheduling of backups, optimizations and repair.

Anti-Spam Plugins

There are several anti-spam plugins available for WordPress, some of the best are:

Akismet

Akismet filters your comments, pingbacks and trackbacks. It performs tests to filter out junk and pushes all spam comments into your spam folder, which you can then review and delete as appropriate.

Defensio

The Defensio web service focuses on threats to social media, such as malicious content, comment spam, and other embedded threats. Defensio also acts as a profanity filter to block bad language in comments.

reCAPTCHA

Even smart spam-bots that use Optical Character Recognition (OCR) to decipher CAPTCHAs cannot get past reCAPTCHA, since the plugin distorts the words to create new images that eliminate spammers.

It is important to make sure all of your plugins are kept up-to-date with the version of WordPress you are running, and that you also keep WordPress updated to the latest build version. This can be verified easily via the WordPress Dashboard, which will notify you if newer versions exist.

Landing Pages

In online marketing, a landing page, sometimes known as a 'lead capture page' or a 'lander', is a single web page that appears in response to clicking on a link from a search engine, social media or email marketing message.

The goal of a landing page is to convert site visitors into sales or leads. A good landing page is designed to get across a particular message regarding your game so those visiting the page will hopefully purchase the game. Landing pages are a great way to present your game professionally, and allow visitors single click access to each of the different stores where your game is available to buy.

Ideally register your game name as a domain, i.e. 'yourgame.com.' If the domain is not available, try the movie trick and register 'yourgamegame. com'. This would be where you host the landing page.

The following checklist is a guide to how you should design an effective landing page:

Single Page Layout

Landing pages should be a single page layout, although you can include navigation to anchors within the page.

Keep It Simple

Keep the page simple and make sure the design is clear and there is minimal clutter onscreen.

Strong Headline

A strong headline, which is engaging and accurately describes what your game is about. You can also include a sub-heading that enforces the message in the headline. Try to use the following words whenever possible:

You—You is a placeholder for your name, making the content feel personal to the reader
Because—Because is an example of 'reason why' advertising—give the reader a good reason why they should buy your game

Prominent Call-to-Action

Call-to-action 'Buy Now' buttons should be positioned near to the top of the page. Use a separate button for each available platform. Make them attention grabbing and a key focal point of the page.

Social Media Icons

Include social icons such as Twitter, Facebook and YouTube, again near to the top of the page.

High Quality Trailer Video

Add a great quality trailer or teaser video. A good place to position the video is just under the Call-to-Action buttons, so visitors can immediately see the game in action. The video is probably the single biggest-selling feature on a landing page.

Action Screenshots

Dynamic screenshots (scrolling, slideshow or selectable); make these the greatest shots from your game, showing the game at its best and most fun.

Explain the Game

Include an interesting and descriptive paragraph about the game, followed by a bullet point features list.

Press Quotes and Review Scores

Prominently display any good reviews or press quotes. You can even work these into the screenshots.

Insider Indie Q&A

1. *What is the name of your studio?*

   Shark Infested Custard Ltd

   shark infested custard ltd

2. *What year was your studio founded and what are the names of the founders?*

   Founded 2013 by Steven Huckle

3. *What are the studio's key game titles?*

   Key/main ambition for the studio is to bring our industry into East Anglia and become a facility to help start and grow new studios in the region. We've been working with the local councils, universities and other groups to open up a studio space where people can have access to tools and people to help them start their own company.

   We also have two projects on the go for large corporations (which I'm not allowed to talk about at the moment); one of them isn't games related, and another title that will be announced soon.

   We're also making some silly, fun things that will be released when they get finished (and the paying work goes quiet).

4. *Do you have your own in-house engine or use a third party system? If third party, which one do you use?*

   90% internal at the moment. Construct 2 and Stencyl are used for prototyping as well as some testing being done in Unity.

5. *Which platforms do you release on now / plan to release on?*

   Win8, iPhone/Pad, Android and PC. In the future we'll hopefully move onto console(s).

6. *Which is your most successful platform so far?*

   No idea . . . yet.

7. *What are the development tools you use most (i.e. 2D, 3D software, audio tools etc.)?*

   Many: Photoshop, 3Ds Max, Maya, After Effects, Construct 2, Visual Studio, Corona, Aseprite, MS Office . . .

   To be honest, there's so much good software out there at the moment (and most of it free/cheap) that we try as many as possible to find the one that's best.

8. *What advice would you give to a new studio?*

   Never underestimate anything: time, people, costs etc.

   Do something that's achievable ('cut your cloth') and within your means and skills.

9. *What marketing resources do you use?*

   None at the moment. Dabbled with twitter and Facebook, but that's about it. Until there's a project in a state, or we're allowed, to show, we're keeping quiet for now.

10. *What are your favourite indie games sites?*

    http://indiegames.com/index.html

    http://britishindie.com

    http://www.indiegamer.com

11. *Any mistakes/hiccups you have made so far, something you would advise a new studio to avoid?*

    A few, but nothing major so far. Over-trusting people/companies/groups too early on and shouting about things before they happened (and then taking 10 times longer than you expect even when taking into account that you expect things to take 10 times longer).

    Make sure people put their money where their mouths are (or wallets), and wait until you see that signature on the dotted line!

    If you need to take on other work to pay the bills and keep going, do it.

    Oh, and make sure your wife understands that you're a little bit mental!

Discussion and Support Forums

Forums, also known as message boards or bulletin boards, are a great way to discuss your games and studio with your community. A forum allows you to get to know your followers much more intimately than the more concise messages on social sites such as Twitter. Forums can be used to provide customer support, track bugs and issues, announce features and even post files and updates.

Be sure to promote the forum on your game press releases and other media, so you can drive traffic to the forum, particularly in the early days. There is nothing worse than an empty forum as it sends out a message that no one is interested in your games, and as a result can actually put people off posting.

Initially you could ask your Twitter and Facebook followers to join the forum, to get a few threads up and running. Post plenty of content yourself; exclusive content can be good to get people interested and involved.

It can be quite hard to get a forum busy with active users. If at first things are quiet, just keep promoting the forum whenever and wherever you can. Keep posting interesting content and engage with anyone who does post, as swiftly as possible.

There are many excellent (and free) forum software packages out there, and I have included the most highly regarded ones below:

Simple Machines Forum
Website: http://www.simplemachines.org

Simple Machines is one of the best forum solutions around. It is very easy to install and there are hundreds of themes and modifications available to download directly from the simplemachines.org site.

phpBB
Website: https://www.phpbb.com

phpBB offers a huge range of features, yet is still easy to set-up and install. I have used phpBB a few times now, and while it is very good, I found many of the themes were often out of date and didn't work as expected. The admin control panel can be a little confusing, with certain functions nested away that should be much more obvious and quicker to access.

Vanilla Forums
Website: http://vanillaforums.org

Vanilla does things very differently to many of the other forum packages, and is particularly well suited to customer-support type discussions. Personally, I really like the different approach Vanilla takes, and it is one of the best for quickly searching and finding specific content thanks to the category and tags system it uses.

MyBB
Website: http://www.mybb.com

MyBB is very similar to phpBB, with a huge selection of free themes and plugins. Apparently MyBB has one of the most advanced plugin systems found in bulletin boards today! Another handy feature is the ability to convert to MyBB from other boards including phpBB, Invision, SMF, PunBB, vBulletin. This makes MyBB a good choice if you want to switch from another BB package.

bbPress
Website: http://bbpress.org

Forum software developed by the creators of WordPress—what more could you want? Configured and set up in much the same way as a WordPress site, this is probably the best option if you are running a forum as part of a WordPress site. A very handy feature is that bbPress uses your existing WordPress theme, so you will have a seamless transition from site to forum.

Source Control

Next up on the list of useful internet-based technologies you shouldn't be without is Source Control.

Source Control (also known as revision control or version control), is the management of changes to source code, art assets, documents and other project data.

Changes are usually identified by a number or letter code, termed the 'revision number', 'revision level', or simply 'revision'. For example, an initial set of files is 'revision 1'. When the first change is made, the resulting set is 'revision 2', and so on. Each revision is associated with a timestamp and the person making the change. Revisions can be compared, restored and with some types of files, merged.

A robust source control system is an absolute necessity to protect your project data. Whatever happens to your local machines, or those of any of the other team members, your data will remain safe and secure.

I firmly believe that you would have to be crazy not to use some form of Source Control. The cost is usually very low, yet the peace of mind is priceless. You also need to find a cheap and reliable hosting company, which offers a lot of storage at low cost. I've always used DreamHost, which seems to give me a never-ending storage supply for seemingly no extra charge.

There are a few different systems out there, but I'll focus on the free options. You really don't need to pay for a Source Control solution when the free options are this good. So let's take a look at the various Source Control platforms out there:

Subversion (SVN)
Website: http://subversion.apache.org

Subversion (SVN) is an open-source version control system. SVN has enjoyed and continues to enjoy widespread adoption in both the open source arena and the corporate world.

I use SVN at Super Icon, and it does everything we need with minimal hassle or quirks. I've had the occasional hiccup with repositories getting slightly out of sync on local machines, but usually the clean-up command fixes this within a few minutes.

You also need to use a client software package to interface between your local machines and SVN, and for this I use Tortoise. Tortoise has gotten better and better over the years; the old niggles are gone, and I find it very reliable. You can download Tortoise for SVN from here: http://tortoisesvn.net.

One downside to SVN is that it is very bad at handling large binary files; I have found that more often than not, if I try to upload lots of large files, SVN fails and I have to retry the upload.

Git
Website: http://git-scm.com

Git is a free and open source distributed version control system designed to handle everything from small to very large projects with speed and efficiency. A huge number of indie projects use Git, and one feature I really like is that you can easily provide external access to Git projects via a web browser.

There is also a version of Tortoise for Git, available from here: https://code.google.com/p/tortoisegit/

Mercurial
Website: http://mercurial.selenic.com

Mercurial is a free, distributed Source Control management tool. It efficiently handles projects of any size and offers an easy and intuitive interface. And, drum roll, there is also a version of Tortoise for Mercurial. Download it from http://tortoisehg.bitbucket.org.

Perforce Platform
Website: http://www.perforce.com/product/perforce

The full Perforce product family (including Swarm) is completely free for up to 20 users and unlimited files. This includes access to their tech support. Crucially, there is no time limit on this free functionality.

Perforce is more often than not the Source Control platform you will find utilized in larger game studios. It is very reliable, fully featured and as it is now free for 20 users, a very good choice for indies.

Plastic SCM
Website: http://www.plasticscm.com/

Plastic SCM is a distributed version control system engineered for companies who require extensive branching and merging, distributed (multi-site/global) scenarios, and/or high performance.

Like Perforce, Plastic SCM is completely free for up to 15 users, and apparently, it is a very good solution for handling large binary files.

CHAPTER **8**
Funding

There are many different funding possibilities available now that game studios can take advantage of, with the choices continually expanding as more and more options become available. Funding is also a very complex area, with each different funding method requiring a significant amount of research and time.

What I have tried to achieve with this chapter is to cover the funding sources that I am aware of, and point you in the direction of further reading and research. You will most likely require specialist professional help to prepare a successful case for funding, although I have put together a quick checklist of points that should help get you started.

Ukie (UK Interactive Entertainment trade body) recently published an excellent guide to accessing finance. Although it focuses on the UK, it is still very informative regardless of where you are based. The report can be found here:

► http://www.ukie.org.uk/a2f

TIGA (the non-profit trade association representing the UK's games industry), as ever, followed suit and have produced

their version too, which is also very good and even more up
to date:

▶ http://www.tiga.org/repository/documents/editorfiles/
onlinesubscribers/tiga_sources_of_finance_document.pdf

An Introduction to Funding

Harry Holmwood, founder and CEO of MAQL Europe, put together
the following pointers on funding. In 1999, Harry founded a software
development studio and took to IPO for $30m. He followed this with
the successful sale of a free online games publisher in 2001. More
recently, in 2008, Harry acted as board director of a motion gaming
company, preparing the sale of the business to a #1 gaming accessories
manufacturer.

So over to Harry, with this great introduction to funding.

External funding can be a good way to help build a game, or a games
business. However, it's not always easy to get and, even if you can get it,
it can come with strings attached that you're not ready for.

Small businesses typically consider three types of funding:

1. Debt Financing—basically, taking a loan from a bank. High Street
    banks are not in the business of making high-risk bets; they like to
    loan money to established, predictable businesses that they can be
    pretty confident they'll get back. If you're making a game, you're not
    that. You won't get a bank loan. Even if you did, you'd have to put
    a personal guarantee on it, which isn't a good idea. So forget bank
    loans.
2. Grants—there are huge numbers of government programs,
    which, particularly in certain locations, can help you with initial
    funding.
3. Investment—this is what we'll look at here.

With investment, someone is putting money into your business in
exchange for a share in the upside. When considering an investment
deal, it's important to see the world from an investor's perspective, so
you can understand what they do and don't want.

An investor looks at a deal from the point of view of risk/reward. How likely is it they will lose some or all of their money? How much money will they make if things go well?

Statistically, an investor putting money into your game or game business is highly likely to lose it all. The riskier the proposition, the higher the potential upside needs to be for them—and the more they're going to want from you in terms of shares or control.

It therefore stands to reason that the more you can reduce the risk, the better the deal you may get from an investor. For example, going to an investor with a finished game, which can be shown to be profitable, seeking money to improve marketing and grow revenues can be seen as pretty low risk. Conversely, a company with no products, and maybe no team, will be seen as ultra high-risk.

The more sophisticated the investor, the tougher they'll be to negotiate with. Broadly, there are three categories of investor you could approach:

Friends and Family

These are people you already know. They're investing in you because they like you, like your idea, and think you could make a go of it. They're likely to be the best source of early finance for most businesses. The downside is—this is real money from real people you have real relationships with. Be very careful about taking investment from friends and relatives without considering "What would this do to my relationship with them if I lost all their money?" Never accept money from friends and relatives that they can't afford to lose.

Angel Investor

This is typically a 'high net worth' (rich) individual. They like investing in businesses for fun and profit. They're more likely to strike a tough deal, but better able to cope with losing money. They may want more shares, or additional control, over your business than friends and family.

Professional Investor

Typically, a venture capital fund (VC) will only invest in established, revenue-generating companies. However, in the tech sector, there are an increasing number of funds able to operate quickly to provide seed capital, usually with very straightforward legal agreements and, particularly in the Bay Area, deal structures that are very attractive to company founders. Currently, though, game companies are not high on professional investor's priorities, as they are seen as too risky and difficult to sustain/grow.

With all investors, the more you can achieve before investment, the better the deal you're likely to achieve. With any investment round, you can expect to give away 20–70% of your company, depending upon the amount of funding sought and how much progress you have made.

Generally, investors want to invest in people and companies, not products. It is unlikely that you will persuade an investor with a compelling game design—with 100 or more games being launched daily, few investors have any ability to determine if one concept or demo is better than any other. Investors care about their exit—how do they get to make a return on their investment? That basically means selling their shares, either by someone buying your company, or by you taking it to IPO.

This last point is the most important of all—once you have investors, you have to realize that their interest is in selling their shares for a profit. So, your personal goals have to align with that. If what you want to do is make a nice living from making great games, because you love games and love making games, you're probably not the right candidate for investment. If your goal is to build a great company, which makes/operates/publishes games, with a view to selling that company at some point in the medium term, the investment route could be right for you. Make sure you are very aware of this—running a company with VC backing, or one on the public markets, is a very different life from making indie games for a living. It can be great fun (I've done both), but it becomes about the growth, the profit, not about the art. Be careful what you wish for!

The best time to raise investment is when you don't need it—if you're running out of cash funding a load of staff and overheads, it's near-impossible to raise money on anything other than the very worst terms. The smartest companies keep their overheads low, achieve something tangible with tiny funding and then use that achievement to market themselves for the next investment round.

Finally, it's incredibly important to realize that getting investment is the start, not the end, of the journey. It's easy, having raised finance, to pat yourself on the back for a job well done when, in fact, the hard work and headaches are only just starting. Go in with your eyes open, and external investment can be the best decision you've ever made. Get it wrong, and it will be the worst.

Find a Mentor

Government services such as Business Link, Business Gateway and BusinessUSA often provide access to mentors, who can be a huge help in preparing documentation to support a funding application. This help can be invaluable, particularly for government-sourced funding. There is usually no fee for using these services, particularly if you are a start-up, and they can make the difference between a successful and an unsuccessful application.

Nesta Games Mentor Network

A new mentoring network, and possibly the best example of its kind in the UK, is the Nesta Games Mentor Network. Established by Ukie and Nesta, specifically to advise and nurture games businesses with an appetite for growth. It was developed from Nesta's already successful Creative Business Mentor Network.

Businesses selected for the new mentoring scheme will receive the following:

► one-to-one business mentoring in the form of 10 two-hour sessions over a 6- to 12-month period;
► an induction workshop at the start of the programme to get the most out of your mentoring sessions;
► workshops and events designed to meet other members of the network; and
► coaching support—in addition to mentoring.

The minimum requirements for joining the scheme are:
► Your business must be registered with Companies House.
► You must have made or sold a game in the UK in the last 12 months or have a game ready to bring to market in the next 6 months.

Alternatively, you can be a business that supports the creation and selling of games that has either launched a product or service in the UK within the last 12 months or intends to launch in the next 6 months. Being a Ukie member automatically qualifies you to apply. If you are interested and would like to find out more, you can email them at cbmn@nesta.org.uk

Attend Events and Meetings

There are many meetings and presentations held covering the various aspects of funding, so try to attend these so you can learn as much information as possible. Network and chat to people at these events; it can be a great way to find people with experience of the whole process. You can also join industry organizations such as Ukie, Tiga and the ESA, who hold regular events covering topics such as funding.

The Due Diligence Process

Many sources of funding will want to perform 'due diligence' on your company before they agree to any funding. This ominous sounding process is designed to verify that what you say about your company is true, and that everything is aboveboard and correct.

The Business Angel defines it this way:

> Due diligence is an investigation or audit of a potential investment, which serves to confirm all material facts. Due diligence refers to the care a reasonable person should take before entering into an agreement or a transaction with another party.
> (http://www.thebusinessangel.org/due-diligence.html)

Due diligence will focus on some or all of the following areas:
- ▶ The team, and in particular the management team's expertise and know-how.
- ▶ Technology: what tech you have in place, is it secure and future proof, what licenced tech is being used etc.
- ▶ Business plan: is it sound, do the figures add up, have you factored in risks, competitors, are the expectations realistic?
- ▶ Development process: your production processes, planning, resources allocation, contingencies and so on.
- ▶ Coding practices: is the game code well designed, flexible, and easy to maintain?
- ▶ Legal checks on the status of the company.

Support Organizations

Ukie
Website: http://ukie.info

Ukie is a trade body for the UK's wider interactive entertainment industry. It exists to champion the interests, needs and positive image of the videogames and interactive entertainment industry.

I asked Ukie for a little more detail on how they can help indie studios. Richie Enticknap had this to say:

> Ukie represents the UK's games and interactive entertainment industry. Our network now consists of nearly 200 UK games businesses, which between them represent the widest possible spectrum of the video games industry. This includes console format holders (Nintendo, Sony, Microsoft as well as new entrants like OUYA); multi-national publishers and lots of developers of all shapes and sizes, from big triple-A types to indie studios and start-up businesses.
>
> We know the challenges facing indie studios and have lots of services that are designed to support, grow and promote our developer members' businesses. We help our developer members in a number of ways such as offering members free or discounted access to international trade events such as GDC San Francisco and Gamescom. As well as running events all around the UK which are free for members and that offer practical and valuable business advice, if you're a member you can also use our free central London hot desks our meeting space whenever you like for your own events and meetings.
>
> We have bespoke discounts and offers on business services for developers to take advantage of such as money off game engines, free legal and financial advice and access to free PR & Marketing expertise to help get your game noticed. We also represent our members' opinions to government and have played a lead role in getting tax breaks for UK games businesses agreed by the UK government (and continue to push them through the European Commission) and getting computer science back onto the national curriculum in this country through our next gen

skills campaign. We work to inspire the next generation of video game talent by running the Video Game Ambassadors scheme alongside STEMnet, which gets industry professionals talking to schoolchildren about potential careers in the industry.

You don't have to be member to get some of the benefits of the Ukie network. For example, we partner with others such as the Indie Games Collective that brought 100 indie developers and Microsoft, Sony and Nintendo together to speak about developing on next-gen consoles. But when you do join Ukie, you become part of a community—our network is your network and we are here to help you get in touch with the people that are vital to your business. Get in touch with us to find out more about all of our events, discounts and other benefits that Ukie membership brings to development businesses.

Tiga
Website: http://www.tiga.org

TIGA is another trade association representing the UK's games industry. Its members include independent games developers, developer-publishers, in-house publisher-owned developers, outsourcing companies, technology businesses and universities. TIGA's vision is to make the UK the best place in the world to do games business.

Note: I realize it is slightly confusing that the UK has what appears to be two near identical industry groups. Which would I recommend? Right now, definitely Ukie.

The Entertainment Software Association (ESA)
Website: http://www.theesa.com/facts

The Entertainment Software Association (ESA) is the US association exclusively dedicated to serving the business and public affairs needs of companies that publish computer and video games for video game consoles, personal computers and the internet.

The Entertainment Software Association of Canada (ESAC)
Website: http://theesa.ca

The voice of the Canadian computer and video game industry that employs approximately 16,500 people at over 325 companies across the country.

IGDA
Website: http://www.igda.org

The International Game Developers Association (IGDA) is the largest non-profit membership organization in the world serving all individuals who create games.

Further Reading

VentureBeat
Website: http://venturebeat.com

VentureBeat covers disruptive technology and explains why it matters in our lives. It is a great place to find a whole range of information about the many aspects of funding. VB also hosts a wealth of general business info relevant to high-tech industries (including games).

TechCrunch
Website: http://techcrunch.com

TechCrunch is a leading technology media property, dedicated to obsessively profiling start-ups, reviewing new internet products and breaking tech news. It is another great source of stories and information about tech start-ups and funding options.

Insider Indie Q&A

1. What is the name of your studio?

Noodlecake Studios

2. *What year was your studio founded and what are the names of the founders?*

    Founded in 2011 by Jordan Schidlowsky and Ty Bader

3. *What are the studio's key game titles?*

    Of our first party games, the Super Stickman Golf series (both 1 and 2) have been huge for us.

4. *Do you have your own in-house engine or use a third party system? If third party, which one do you use?*

    Combination thereof. We have some custom tools we use for porting iOS games to Android as well we use a variety of things like Cocos2D, Unity etc. for our games.

5. *Which platforms do you release on now / plan to release on?*

    Currently we release on iOS, Android, Amazon and have some titles on OUYA and even Roku and Blackberry. We are in the process of expanding; however, I can't get into the details just yet.

6. *Which is your most successful platform so far?*

    iOS traditionally has been the most successful in terms of straight-out money, however Android is catching up rapidly. Additionally, we have many more users on Android, so there is a value in that.

7. *What are the development tools you use most (i.e. 2D, 3D software, audio tools etc.)?*

    As mentioned above we use Cocos2D and Unity for most of our projects at this point. In addition to some tools such as Matt Rix's Futile engine for Unity.

8. *What advice would you give to a new studio?*

    Don't be afraid of hard work. We had to put in a lot of hours to get where we are at today and overnight success is a rarity. Most developers who seem to pop up out of nowhere have actually been working hard for a long time. Also don't be afraid to ask for help. The indie community is a very open and collaborative space filled with developers who are willing to lend you a hand.

9. *What marketing resources do you use?*

    We use a combination of things. First, of course we pound the pavement at conferences making connections and talking with gamers about what we are doing. Then, of course, social media comes into play and a good relationship with editors at gaming publications. Last, we cross-promote internally and externally with other developers.

10. *What are your favourite indie games sites?*

    Tough to just pick one. Touch Arcade, IGN, Polygon, Giant Bomb, Indiegames.com, 148Apps, Gamasutra, PocketGamer and more are all

> great for games coverage and all offer different things. So, it really depends what you are looking for.
>
> 11. *Any mistakes/hiccups you have made so far, something you would advise a new studio to avoid?*
>
> We have made a ton of mistakes up to this point and it is hard to pick just one. But that is ok, and leads into the advice I would give developers, which is don't be afraid to make them. That is the only way you will learn and become a better developer and company. Some things that sound great on paper might end up not going over well with users and trust me, they will let you know. But take that feedback and use it to grow from.

Sources of Funding

Early Access/Alpha Funding

Early Access/Alpha funding is an increasingly popular way to help fund indie game development. It isn't right for every game though, and certain genres are much better suited to this type of funding. Sandbox games are a good fit for Alpha funding as players anticipate a fairly open specification in the early stages, and expect that their feedback will help shape the game during the course of development.

The primary risk for Early Access funding is failure to impress the community, which could kill interest in the game before you even release. Make sure you get your pricing right too—you really shouldn't ever charge more for Early Access than for final release. The community playing your Early Access build is helping you and as such they need to be respected and not overcharged.

The mighty Minecraft offers a good reference point here. It was initially released as a free demo/pre-Alpha and then increased in price over time: $10-$15 during Alpha, $20 during Beta, and is currently $26.95.

Ensure you get the core game features in there before you release an Early Access. Any features that are part of your USP list should certainly be in there, and properly implemented at that. Early Access funding offers a great opportunity to get people passionate about your game early on, but you have to go into it with an open mind and be receptive to ideas and criticism from the community. As Minecraft's creator

Markus 'Notch' Persson says, "Let their feedback influence your list of planned features and take on board popular ideas. But at the same time, keep to the principles of your core game idea. Immerse yourself into the community, even if there are bad spots. The good times are good! Support the YouTubers and streamers as they are your lifeblood. Modding is awesome."

"Alpha funding your game can also help with marketing," he adds, "as it can draw in a large crowd of players who spread the word through social media channels and their friends."

Another point Persson makes is "Be clear. Absolutely, unambiguously, massively clear on what it is your game is offering today, what you're planning to add in the near future and what your vision is for your game."

Try to make sure you release regular updates to keep up interest in your game and engage with the community in an open, honest and non-defensive way.

A recent story of an amazingly successful Early Access funding campaign is the game Prison Architect by British developers Introversion. Before the Alpha was released, Introversion were nearly bankrupt, the owners wracked with worries over money. Yet they managed to turn things around in epic fashion with Prison Architect. The Alpha build was initially sold directly via Introversion's own site, later joining the first batch of Steam Early Access games. With regular monthly patches adding major new features and regular devblogs to update the community, along with a Kickstarter style pricing structure, the Prison Architect Alpha shot into orbit, earning Introversion several million dollars of revenue!

Abertay University Prototype Fund

Website: http://prototypefund.abertay.ac.uk

Abertay University provides grants of up to £25,000 for small companies (based anywhere in the UK, unless otherwise stated in calls for region-specific applications) that are developing their own games or other forms of interactive digital content.

Abertay University does not take ownership of any IP or equity created during the project.

To apply you will need to monitor the Abertay website as they organise the applications process into rounds, and you can only apply when a round is open. The Prototype Fund looks for:

Innovation

Your project should have an aspect of competitive advantage within the market. We're not only looking for a great idea, but implementation and execution too.

Route to Market

Your project should have a clear route to market. Demonstrate how you plan to secure funds to complete development and launch the product.

Commercial Viability

Your project should be commercially strong enough to generate sufficient revenue to grow your business.

Development Capability

Show us that your team can develop and deliver the prototype to the set budget and timescales. Detailed planning is the key here.

Business Scalability and Capacity

Your business should be able to grow and strengthen, forming a long-term co-located team or studio. Single-person developers and dispersed teams please take note.

Business Angels

Business angels are wealthy individuals who invest in start-up and growth companies in return for equity in the company. This investment can involve both time and money depending upon how hands-on the investor wishes to be. It can be a very positive thing if the investor is willing to put their time into a business, you can learn a lot from them and it could really help open doors for additional help and funding rounds in the future.

Typically, business angels have already made their fortune through other business ventures, possibly their own start-up or a career in business. They can operate independently or as a syndicate. Angels funding as part of a group enables them to pool their finances and their skills, although usually there is a lead angel who will act on behalf of the syndicate.

One key point to remember before approaching an angel is that they will be looking for the possibility of a high return (usually an expected average annual return of at least 20–30% per annum). Most of this return will be realised in the form of capital gains over a period of several years. They will also expect an exit from your business within five to eight years, so you will need to show a realistic growth plan.

London Business Angels
Website: http://www.lbangels.co.uk

London Business Angels (LBA) is one of Europe's leading Angel Investment Networks. They connect innovating fast growth technology companies to equity finance through their membership of experienced angel investors.

UK Business Angels Association
Website: http://www.ukbusinessangelsassociation.org.uk

The UK Business Angels Association is the national trade association representing angel and early stage investment in the UK.

American Angels Association
Website: http://www.americanangelsassociation.com

American Angels Association put business angel investors in touch with ventures seeking funding across the United States of America.

National Angel Capital Association
Website: https://nacocanada.com

The National Angel Capital Organization (NACO) accelerates a thriving, early-stage investing ecosystem in Canada by connecting individuals, groups and other partners that support Angel-stage investing.

Indie Fund
Website: http://indie-fund.com

Indie Fund is a funding source for independent developers, created by a group of successful indies looking to encourage the next wave of game developers. It was established as a serious alternative to the traditional , publisher-funding model. Their aim is to support the growth of games as a medium by helping indie developers get (and stay) financially independent.

Venture Capital

A Venture Capitalist (VC) invests money in a company that is high risk and has the possibility of high growth in return for often-substantial equity in the company. VCs usually also insist on significant control over company decisions once they invest. VC funding can be a good fit with games, as they are usually most interested in businesses in high technology industries, such as biotechnology, IT and software.

Typically, the funding is for start-up or expansion, and the investment is usually for a period of five to seven years. At the end of the investment period, the investor will expect a return on their money either by the sale of the company or by floating the company and selling shares to the public. VCs are looking for a higher rate of return than would be given by more traditional investments, typically a minimum of a 25% return.

VCs can be risk averse and you would need to show without doubt that your company has high growth prospects, and is managed by an experienced and ambitious team who are capable of turning their business plan into reality.

VCs typically invest in businesses with a minimum need of around £2 million (though many smaller organisations do exist who invest lesser amounts). You will most certainly need a proven track record in one form or another (i.e. previously involved in the creation of a very successful hit game).

British Private Equity & Venture Capital Association (BVCA)
Website: http://www.bvca.co.uk

The British Private Equity & Venture Capital Association (BVCA) is the industry body and public policy advocate for the private equity and venture capital industry in the UK.

National Venture Capital Association (NVCA)
Website: http://www.nvca.org

The National Venture Capital Association (NVCA) empowers its members and the entrepreneurs they fund by advocating for policies that encourage innovation and reward long-term investment.

Canada's Venture Capital & Private Equity Association
Website: http://www.cvca.ca

The CVCA—Canada's Venture Capital & Private Equity Association—represents the majority of private equity companies in Canada, with over 2000 members. CVCA members have over $105 billion in capital under management.

Digital Capital

Website: http://www.digitalcapital.ch

Digital Capital is a bit of a newcomer, offering a different sort of deal. Rather than funding your existing company/start up, you would become a partner in a new foreign corporation which would develop your idea into a commercially viable product. This new company would hold all ownership, title, trademark, intellectual property rights, royalties etc. to the resulting product.

Digital Capital fund a variety of projects including video games and interactive software on mobile devices, Smart TV, consoles and PC.

So it's quite a unique approach, and with their focus on digitally distributed projects and strong links to the game industry, they could certainly be an option to consider.

Game Incubators and Accelerators

Incubators and accelerators help start-ups build and develop their product, business models and marketing strategies. They will usually provide free office/studio space, software and hardware to enable start-ups to hit the ground running. Some provide seed funding, while others focus more on connecting studios with funding partners, angels and VCs. Typically, you will also gain access to partnership deals that can help support the various aspects of developing and publishing a game.

Execution Labs

Website: http://executionlabs.com/en
Area: Montreal, Canada

Execution Labs help independent game developers produce the games they want to make and then we help them bring those games to market. The goal is to enable experienced developers to become true entrepreneurs and pursue their dreams of creative independence.

YetiZen

Website: http://yetizen.com
Area: San Francisco, USA

The YetiZen Accelerator Program is focused entirely on game studio and emerging platform start-ups. It includes access to their 20,000 square feet games innovation space in the heart of San Francisco.

RocketSpace

Website: http://rocket-space.com
Area: San Francisco, USA

RocketSpace is an accelerator for high-growth, seed-funded tech start-ups. They will, for the right start-ups, 'provide the fuel' needed to accelerate growth. This includes access to top talent, tier 1 venture capital and blue-chip brands representing millions of potential customers.

Games Ireland
Website: http://gamesireland.ie/wordpress/gamesireland
Area: Dublin, Ireland

Games Ireland is an advocacy group that unifies the Irish games sector and drives sustainable growth in the industry at a crucial time for this country. We are especially focused on representing Ireland's growing indigenous industry providing structural support and promoting a conducive environment for funding and investment.

The Digit Incubator
Website: http://digitgaming.com/incubator
Area: Dublin, Ireland

The Digit Incubator gives Irish game start-ups the best start they can get as they bring exciting new games to market across all platforms. The purpose-built games environment combined with access to the Digit team and a wider cohort of industry executives makes this a unique offering for the sector in Ireland.

HouseOGames
Website: http://houseogames.com
Area: Seattle, USA

The unique living and work space that HouseOGames provides enables indie developers to prototype, design, play test and ultimately release to market. HouseOGames has over 40 mentors covering a vast amount of industry knowledge, from platforms and marketing to production and business to help guide our teams to success.

Game Founders
Website: http://www.gamefounders.com
Area: Estonia

A game incubator which offers three months of free office space in a 'cool, brand-new' building in Tallinn.

Game CoLab
Website: http://www.gamecolab.org
Area: Phoenix, USA

Game CoLab is a non-profit organization that acts as the advocate for the game community in Arizona.

Bristol Games Hub
Website: http://bristolgameshub.com/about
Area: Bristol, UK

Bristol Games Hub is a non-profit organisation that provides working space in Bristol where game developers and academics come together under one roof to create and study games.

Crowdfunding

Crowdfunding (also known as Crowdsourcing) is a way of raising finance by asking a large number of people each for a small amount of money.

The most common method of Crowdfunding for games is the All-or-Nothing model. A target goal is set for the required level of investment within a time limit (usually 30 days). When the fund-raising period is over, pledged money is only collected from the contributors if the fund-raising goal is met. If the goal is not met, no money is collected.

If you are planning a Crowdfunding campaign, you need to spend plenty of time on research. It is an incredibly intense experience; those 30 days will be about the busiest of your career, so you have to make sure you go in fully prepared.

The following tips are from Jay Koottarappallil, CEO of WhiteMoon Dreams. WhiteMoon recently ran a successful Kickstarter for their game WARMACHINE: Tactics, earning pledges of $1,578,950.

1. Do your research. Research other Kickstarters, research your genre, research your genre's demographic. Use this information to put together a scenario of what you can reasonably raise. Shoot for less than this as your starting ask.
2. Your base offering should be BARE Minimum Viable Product*. If the concept is good, people will fund the stretch goals to build out the vision.
3. Build a community BEFORE you launch the Kickstarter. Do whatever you need to in order to get people excited here, but don't launch into an empty void. That community will create the initial surge, which will start the Kickstarter snowball. And in case you didn't notice, Kickstarter IS a snowball. The idea can be good, bad

or mediocre, but if it picks up a lot of steam initially, it will most likely fund.

4. Stay in constant contact with the community during the Kickstarter. Updates, chatting in comments, anything. Don't sleep. Don't stay away from the computer for more than an hour. Be around and show them that you care about them and you're going to put this kind of care into the thing you're making for them.

5. If you are a game developer and you aren't some huge famous name, do NOT approach Kickstarter without a version of the game that you can at least demonstrate on video. Paper pitches suck in any form. The game MUST be playable.

*A Minimum Viable Product has just those features that allow the product to be deployed, and no more. The product is typically deployed to a subset of possible customers, such as early adopters that are thought to be more forgiving, more likely to give feedback and able to grasp a product vision from an early prototype or marketing information.

The following list includes the best-known and most popular Crowdfunding sites for games:

IndieGogo
Website: www.indiegogo.com

You can raise money for anything on IndieGogo, including for-profit ventures, creative ideas or personal needs. No matter where you live, you can start your campaign and collect money from any country in the world as long as you have a valid bank account.

IndieGogo is a very popular choice for game developers, although it seems to be a little less effective than Kickstarter at successfully funding projects.

Kickstarter
Website: www.kickstarter.com

A home for everything from films, games and music to art, design and technology. Kickstarter is full of projects, big and small, that are brought to life through the direct support of people like you.

Kickstarter is the crowdfunding platform for games. It is regarded as the first choice for crowdfunding a game and has seen many successful game projects.

Equity Crowdfunding

Another approach to Crowdfunding is equity Crowdfunding, whereby individuals who are willing to invest do so in exchange for equity in the business. This type of Crowdfunding is more likely to be used to finance business growth, rather than individual products, and can be a good option to consider to expand your studio. There are many equity Crowdfunding sites out there; a good example is CrowdCube (http://www.crowdcube.com).

VentureBeat is a good place to start in the search for equity Crowdfunding resources.

Insider Indie Q&A

1. *What is the name of your studio?*

   WhiteMoon Dreams

2. *What year was your studio founded and what are the names of the founders?*

   Founded 2007 by Jay Koottarappallil, Robert Scott Campbell, Kevin Mack and Norvell Thomas Jr.

3. *What are the studio's key game titles?*

   Our first game actually is our big one—WARMACHINE: Tactics

4. *Do you have your own in-house engine or use a third party system? If third party, which one do you use?*

   We have used nearly every engine available to man and have finally settled into Unreal 4

5. *Which platforms do you release on now / plan to release on?*

   Our key platforms are actually PC, then Xbox One/PS4 and then mobile devices.

6. *Which is your most successful platform so far?*

   We haven't released our game yet, but it will likely be PC

7. *What are the development tools you use most (i.e. 2D, 3D software, audio tools etc.)?*

   Visual Studio 2012, MS Office, Autodesk Maya, 3DSMax, Zbrush, XNormal, Photoshop, Painter, Sony Vegas and Sound Forge

8. *What advice would you give to a new studio?*

   ► Never, ever give up.
   ► Failure is just as imminent as success is. Prepare for nothing else other than to push forward in all cases.
   ► Don't get stuck doing something just to pay the bills. Always be working on your original goal even if you're having to do it around the work that pays the bills. Just don't stop doing it or it's very unlikely that it will become the focus of your company and you will never achieve the goal without major course correction.
   ► Surround yourself with people who inspire you and do everything you can to keep them. Work only with people you adore. For all intents and purposes, they are an extension of your family.
   ► Rally around your project. Sure, money is a great motivator, but nothing motivates people like seeing their project come together. Make sure every team member constantly sees what's going on with the whole project and call out the accomplishments of the different groups on the team. It's very easy for a team to collectively lose focus when individuals can't see how their work contributes to a whole.

9. *What marketing resources do you use?*

   We use various PR firms. Marketing isn't as effective for us as PR is. We also leverage our growing community and give them the resources and ability to grow it themselves.

10. *What are your favourite indie games sites?*

    Actually, it's not an indie games site per se, but I pick up so much from Humble Bundle and I'm turned on to new things by what I see there.

11. *Any mistakes/hiccups you have made so far, something you would advise a new studio to avoid?*

  ▶ Settle on tech solutions that you believe in early on. We spent too much time courting various solutions even though we knew what we really wanted to use. We didn't use the solution we wanted because it was too expensive, but in the end, all the wasted time with tech that didn't work out was more expensive.
  ▶ Do business ONLY with people you are ridiculously excited to do business with. We kind of courted everyone in order to figure out which ones were possible opportunities, but the only ones that ended up mattering were the ones that we were the most excited about. Everything else was a waste of time for biz dev.
  ▶ We have been screwed over by folks bigger than us that didn't feel like they wanted to honour the contract because they were done with our services. Our mistake was to not have multiple streams of revenue when we were not independently funded. Don't put all your eggs in one basket. Even after you land one deal, get working on the next one, unless you're paying yourself.
  ▶ Be very careful about assigning leadership. We thought we could assign leadership based on evaluating other peoples' performance at different companies, seniority etc. but in the end this rarely worked out. Leadership is born through folks working together. Good leaders are excellent communicators first and everything else second.
  ▶ OMG I could probably go on forever here . . .

Games Publishers

The game publisher role has changed a lot recently due to digital distribution and the high number of developers self-publishing their games. Mid–low tier publishers have just about been wiped out, which is good in that there are now less sharks out there, but bad in another way as it limits publisher-funding options.

To stand a chance of attracting a publisher to fund your original IP, you will typically need to be talking AAA standard now, or an amazingly strong and original indie title.

Publisher funding can still be a great way to build up a team, but keep your eye on the bigger picture and don't become over-reliant on publisher funding. It can often be very hard to secure follow-up projects unless you have a huge hit, and many studios have fallen after completing a game and failing to get a new deal in place.

Platform Holders

Platform holders, and in particular Sony, often offer funding for exclusive titles on their platforms. Sony really started to do this with PSP Minis titles, to boost the number of titles on the service, and now more recently with PlayStation Mobile, Vita and PS4 indie games.

The beauty of this is that they will also help to promote your game, as it is in both of your interests for a funded title to do well. You are assigned an account manager who is there to help throughout the whole process, and you are assured a quick response to any issues or queries.

Nintendo are now also very approachable and indie friendly. While there are not so many funding opportunities, they may well help with loan kits and marketing support.

Development Grants

Wherever your region, there are usually government supported grants available for certain aspects of your business. These may be game specific, job creation, start-up grants or any number of other options.

A local business support service would be your first point of call here, as they can advise on whether you would be eligible for any of the available grants. They will often help you to prepare the paperwork, particularly for the non-industry-specific grants.

Game friendly / specific funds include:

Nordic Game Fund
Website: http://www.nordicgameprogram.org

Canada Media Fund
Website: http://www.cmf-fmc.ca/?setLocale=1

Creative England
Website: http://www.creativeengland.co.uk/index.php/portfolio/funding

Regional Growth Funds

A subset of government funding, regional funds are often available to fund business start-ups and job creation in specific local areas, such as areas where the traditional local industry has been lost and the government is trying to attract new industries to the area.

This is a huge area, so you will need to research what is available locally to you—by way of an example, here is a link to the UK Regional Growth Fund (RGF):
Website: https://www.gov.uk/understanding-the-regional-growth-fund

Festivals and Contest Prizes

There are an ever-increasing number of festivals and contests open to indie developers, often with cash prizes. The IGF is the most popular, while other popular ones include IndieCade and Create Something Unreal. While the prizes are often small, any extra money is always a bonus, and perhaps more importantly, it can give your game a boost.

Production Tax Credits

The aim of tax credit relief is to promote sustainable production of video games within a region, to assist in job creation and often to promote culturally significant aspects of the area. Qualifying studios are able to claim tax breaks on expenditure spent on the development of a video game intended for the public.

Most payroll tax credits and rebates only cover wages paid to residents and do not allow for non-resident salaries. The expenditure incurred in the design, production and testing of the video game must be locally directed. Finally, the company seeking relief must be a company incorporated and run from the country of application.

There can be minimum and/or maximum limits on the size of the projects that can be funded. Some incentives are designed for games with large teams and long development times, while others are designed to support much smaller projects.

The recent UK tax relief scheme allows companies to claim 25% of qualifying games production expenditure as a corporation tax credit, with no minimum or maximum expenditure. Quebec in Canada offers a 30% tax relief on salaries and production costs. France provides a 20% production tax credit on games that pass a cultural test. Several states in the USA now offer games tax credits.

Where a game must satisfy a cultural test, you usually have to score over a certain amount of points to qualify. The majority of these points are awarded if the game is developed locally and is produced in the language of the region.

Research and Development (R&D) Tax Credits

Another relief scheme that many governments operate is R&D tax credits. The objective is to use tax incentives to encourage technical firms to invest in developing their own innovative products, thus encouraging more investment in this kind of innovation.

R&D tax credits are a company tax relief that can either reduce a company's tax bill or, for some small- or medium-sized companies, provide a cash sum. For example, in the UK the R&D tax credit works by allowing companies to deduct up to 225% of qualifying expenditure on R&D activities when calculating their profit for tax purposes. Companies that are SMEs can, in certain circumstances, surrender this tax relief to claim payable tax credits in cash from HM Revenue & Customs.

Providing you prepare the paperwork correctly, most game studios are likely to be eligible for R&D tax credits. The type of R&D you can claim can include:

▶ Overcome the limitations of current technology, development environments and mobile devices—such as small screen sizes, limitations in memory, performance restrictions.
▶ Develop more effective game and rendering engines.
▶ Improve the speed with which games perform on a variety of platforms.
▶ Porting a game to a new technology and/or hardware platform. This could also be extended to include the resolution of compatibility issues relating to operating games across multiple platforms.

To make a successful R&D tax credits claim you will most likely need to use a company who specializes in R&D submissions for games. You have to be very specific to work within the rules set by the various tax departments. In the UK, JumpStart and Myriad seem to be the most popular choices for games developers:

JumpStart
Website: www.jumpstartuk.co.uk

Myriad Associates
Website: http://www.myriadassociates.com

Insider Indie Q&A

1. What is the name of your studio?

Engine Software BV

2. What year was your studio founded and what are the names of the founders?

1995 by myself, Ivo Wubbels, Falco Dam and Jeroen Schmitz . . . typical 'in-the-attic' start-up (ok it was a spare bedroom in Ivo's parents' house)

3. What are the studio's key game titles?

We have a smash-hit right now with Terraria on consoles (and soon Vita), and previously we had some relatively successful properties like Just SING! (on Nintendo DS, spawned four games) and we worked on the hugely successful PuzzleQuest DS (although that was work-for-hire). Our biggest success will be our next game—as it should be.

4. Do you have your own in-house engine or use a third party system? If third party, which one do you use?

It totally depends. We use both our own custom tech (for DS, 3DS, PS3, Xbox360, Vita) and third-party tools, mainly Unity (for iOS, Android).

5. Which platforms do you release on now / plan to release on?

Every (currently we have games out or in development for PS3, X360, XBO, PS4, Vita, DS, 3DS, Wii, Wii-U, iOS and Android)

6. Which is your most successful platform so far?

Nintendo DS without a doubt (over 50 games developed)

7. *What are the development tools you use most (i.e. 2D, 3D software, audio tools etc.)?*

Photoshop and 3D Studio Max for graphics, Audition and SONAR (+libs) for audio, Visual Studio for coding

8. *What advice would you give to a new studio?*

I would give each studio specific advice based on their own skill sets (and mainly lacking skill sets). Having worked with other indie studios, the most creative ones lack direction, the better managed ones lack creativity . . . it is not mutually exclusive, thank God, but I guess the most common mistake is thinking you need no direction whatsoever. Which is false. Productive creativity needs focus and boundaries.

9. *What marketing resources do you use?*

Written press, e-zines, viral marketing and social platforms. For most indies, having a blog, forum and YouTube channel can get you really far.

10. *What are your favourite indie games sites?*

Not just indie, but Gamasutra has always been awesome. Reddit can make a huge impact; I also regularly browse through indiedb.com.

11. *Any mistakes/hiccups you have made so far, something you would advise a new studio to avoid?*

I think in the 17 years in business we have made every mistake possible. Getting too stuck on a specific game design idea even though it really doesn't work the way you had hoped. Thinking "it works for me, so it works for everyone," financially bad decisions, over-specialization. Underestimating marketing, underestimating community interaction, underestimating the time needed to develop something . . . There are way more pitfalls than correct paths. But hey, we are still here.

CHAPTER **9**
Tax, Legal and Other Odds and Ends

And here we are, the last chapter of the book! I hope you have found the book useful so far. For this last chapter I have included anything else I could think of that isn't covered by the other sections of the book. So we have legal stuff, intellectual property, copyright, withholding taxes, legal text and agency representation.

I realise that this last chapter is a slight mish-mash of stuff, but I wanted to make sure I didn't leave anything out. Let's start by looking at your most important asset, your intellectual property (IP). Always look after and treasure your IP, as it is by far the most valuable aspect of any games business.

Looking After Your IP

Hopefully, most indie studios know the value of IP; without developing and maintaining your own IP it is fairly unlikely you will be able to sustain a business longer term. IP refers to creations of the mind, such as inventions, literary and artistic works, designs, and symbols, names and images used in commerce.

Also, make sure that anyone who undertakes any work for you assigns the entire IP rights to your studio. If they do not do this, they will retain the IP rights and this can lead to all sorts of problems later. Never leave this to chance as that can be a recipe for disaster, causing you many problems, and a potential world of pain if it turns out a contractor isn't all they seem. Get an agreement in place from day one!

Agreements have to be in writing and signed by all parties involved. Another necessity is a robust confidentiality clause, to prevent any confidential information being disclosed without your permission.

Alex Chapman, a partner in the Computer Games and Digital Media Groups at Sheridans, has the following very useful advice on the various rights associated with computer game development and production:

Identifying Rights in Interactive Media Businesses

From the moment a developer comes up with a concept to the moment a product is launched (and beyond) valuable rights are being created.

The players in the video games industry and similar businesses depend on these intangible assets—known to lawyers as 'Intellectual Property Rights'. It is in these rights that many businesses find their value and nowadays it is the intellectual capital of a company that will often determine whether it represents a good investment and viable business partner. This is particularly important now that the inability to secure additional funding is forcing many companies to fold.

In contrast, businesses that are conscious of their properties and rights are flourishing. This is not a difficult position to achieve but to do so you need to identify what these rights are, where they exist and how they arise.

These rights take a number of different forms, the most important of which (from the point of view of creative business) is copyright.

What Rights?—Copyright

An initial idea is not rich in intellectual property—it is difficult to protect and difficult to value. However, as soon it is translated into a physical form—either by way of storyboard, written design specification or hard code—the most basic intellectual property right exists, that being copyright.

As a rule of thumb, copyright exists in all original creative works—hence copyright exists in original designs, video footage, the sequence of a story board, software code, in-game text, music and so on.

Where?—Copyright

Copyright works are everywhere. All artistic, literary and musical works attract protection so long as they are original. Copyright cannot, however, exist in the following:

1. single words and names;
2. a process, e.g. means of making something; or
3. an idea, unless it expresses a tangible form and that tangible form has copyright.

How and Who—Copyright

Copyright arises on the creation of the work. It is instant and does not require registration or any additional formality. The more important question is who created the work and who owns it. This is of fundamental importance for businesses and the development of their assets.

The general rule is that the creator is the first owner—though there are a few exceptions. The first is that employees do not own the copyright in work they create in the course of their employment. This is of crucial importance to the games industry and must be distinguished from the frightening reality that works created by a person who is not an actual employee will belong to that person NOT the person paying for the work. If that is the case for some of your works, you are unlikely to own the copyright in them but may have an implied licence to use for a limited purpose.

This is alarming and can only be circumvented by something expressed in writing to the contrary and signed by the creator before or after the work is done. All freelancers working for developers should therefore have written agreements transferring rights to the commissioner. If you have these—or get them—then you will have built (or will build) your asset base.

Other Rights

Identification of rights doesn't end with copyright. The other areas to look out for are:

1. Trademark rights
2. Patent rights

3. Database rights
4. Image and personality rights
5. Third-party licences
6. Know-how and confidential information

The golden rule with these, like copyright, is to record in a single location which of these rights you own.

Investors like to see what you own. They are interested in models, business plans and projections etc., but they need to know what it is they are actually investing in and what the company has and what the company will have. For creative businesses these rights are its assets and when we conduct due diligence on companies, we look principally to see what these rights are—because it is on these foundations that all creative businesses rest.

Taking the above in turn:
1. Trademark rights

I explained earlier that there is no copyright in a name or word. There are, however, trademark rights both registered and unregistered in words, logos and various other devices "capable of graphic representation." Such rights protect the goodwill and reputation in your business.

Unregistered rights are not easily enforceable but they have value, as they may give rise to claims in "passing off"—for example if a third party does something the same or similar and in doing so misrepresents itself, creates confusion and causes damage. The value in unregistered marks lies in these rights.

Registered marks are more easily enforceable and therefore instantly more valuable. So every work, slogan, device, logo, name etc. you have used in the course of your business has potential trademark rights. Protecting these rights is dealt with in the next issue but by identifying them now you will be identifying assets with value. Once you know what you have, you can then decide whether they are worth protecting further.

2. Patent rights

If you have something that is inventive and not in the public domain but capable of industrial application, then you may be entitled to apply for a patent. These are not cheap, with worldwide programmes costing around £100,000. However to preserve these rights prior to your application, you must keep the details confidential—and if you haven't done so already the chances are you will have lost them.

3. Database rights

This right is similar to copyright but exists in relation to the compilation of data. For example, the database compiled and owned by the developer of a football management game has value within the game itself and in that it may be licensed to others. Accordingly, it needs protection against wholesale copying by others.

There are other examples. Database right will exist in the new ELSPA book and any other directory as well as CTW's list of developers on its website. This right isn't lost just because it is published and anyone using that database for a commercial purpose should pay a licence fee to the owner.

Identifying where this right exists gives you the opportunity to identify another source of revenue. It is however important to make sure that the collected data is accurate with the necessary data protection consents.

4. Image and personality rights

Personality rights present a number of problems for media businesses wishing to use or make reference to individuals as part of their product. They are unlikely to be an asset to a business unless a third-party licence can be established (see below).

I have recently drafted agreements between a number of well-known footballers and their website providers in relation to the use of their personality rights. These contracts are clearly valuable to both parties as are the rights that go with them.

The other area where personality rights may exist is within the industry itself. Bill Gates, for example, has value in his name and face, adding value to the balance sheet of Microsoft, and if the CEO or lead programmer of your business is such a person, there may be some justification in adding that to the intellectual capital of the business.

5. Third-party licences

Licences in and out represent valuable uses of intellectual property. They are commonplace particularly as they have a calculable revenue stream. They may also represent intellectual capital and should be valued as such. Third-party licences in characters, existing franchises and similar contracts add value to a company now and provide further opportunities for the future.

6. Know-how and confidential information

Confidential information and trade secrets can have huge value and should not be underestimated. The confidential information can be a business method, process or a formula—for example the Coca-Cola and KFC recipes. These add structure and value to your business.

Setting them out and coordinating them adds value and gives you opportunity to license that know-how. That is how franchises are built. I am presently advising a number of clients who are looking to license their know-how and brand worldwide. They are already able to do so and by realising they may, then they add a valuable income stream in addition to their core business.

Advice

Identifying a business's intellectual property rights is fundamental to realising its value. Businesses should therefore:

- ▶ Conduct an audit of all your creative works, know how, marks, and properties as described above.
- ▶ Establish who created them, when and on what terms.
- ▶ Catalogue all rights you now own.
- ▶ Continue the cataloguing process in future.

A big thanks to Alex for those very useful insights. I've used Sheridans many times in the past for legal advice, and can thoroughly recommend them, regardless of your studio size.

IP Holding Companies

Many large corporations and businesses operate dedicated IP holding companies. A holding company is a separate entity that owns the intellectual property assets of the group, and then licenses these to affiliated companies as needed for their use. The reasons for adopting such a structure are varied, ranging from the ability to more easily manage the IP portfolio, protecting your IP from legal claims, to beneficial tax treatment that may be obtained in some jurisdictions.

You need to establish the holding company early in the development of your intellectual property, i.e. before the IP has significant value (presumably prior to commercialization). Once IP rights are transferred, you usually pay royalties to the holding company in exchange for use of the IP; note that it is wise to set a royalty rate as if it were between third parties in an arm's-length transaction.

If your IP is separate from your main trading company, this offers significant protection for your IP in the event of legal action, or in the event of the trading company entering into administration.

Where to Base?

You can set up a holding company in your own jurisdiction, which is usually fine for smaller companies. You can also establish the holding company in a separate country entirely. This can be a little daunting, and a lot more expensive, but providing you are transparent with your local tax authority it is all perfectly legal and above board.

Some of the best locations to base a holding company are:
- Austria
- Belgium
- Denmark
- Hong Kong
- Luxemburg
- Malta
- Netherlands
- Norway
- Sweden
- Switzerland
- UK

If you shop around you can find some very reasonable company formation packages. One final word—this is a very complex area and you really must seek professional advice.

Withholding Taxes

If you self-publish and plan to release in different regions, you should be aware of source withholding taxes. Fortunately, all of the platform holders provide online access to the various forms that you need to complete. It is very important that you fill these out correctly so as to avoid tax withholding.

As an example, royalty payments earned in the US by a foreign company are subject to a source withholding tax as high as 30%. Fortunately, most countries have tax treaties with the US in place, so providing you take the necessary steps, you can eliminate this tax. I've detailed the steps below for compliance with the US IRS.

1. You need to obtain an EIN number, which is incredibly easy to do. You should call this number: 001-215-516-6999, which is a dedicated line for foreign businesses requiring EIN numbers. They will ask your business name, address and one or two other details, and you'll get the number over the phone with a copy sent out by post a week or so later. **Note:** This is no longer required by some of the platform holders.
2. Next, you need to complete IRS form W-8BEN. A point of note is that it is the download service providers who will collect the tax on behalf of the IRS, for example, Nintendo for the eShop, Apple for iPhone etc., so you may need to supply the completed form to them.

Insider Indie Q&A

1. What is the name of your studio?

Bossa Studios

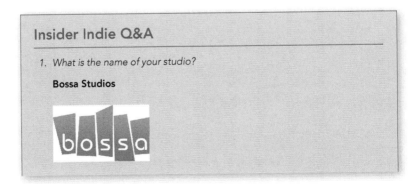

2. *What year was your studio founded and what are the names of your founders?*

   We founded Bossa Studios in 2010. The founding partners working for Bossa are Roberta Lucca, Henrique Olifiers and Imre Jele.

3. *What are the studio's key game titles?*

   We've worked on a range of games, but Bossa is probably most known for two games.

   Monstermind was our first game and it went on to win a BAFTA. We often described it as an "antisocial game" as it allowed players to build the city of their dreams, and then send B-movie inspired monsters to destroy the cities of their friends.

   Our latest game, Surgeon Simulator is a darkly humorous over-the-top operation sim game where players become Nigel Burke, a would-be surgeon taking life into his own shaky hands, performing life-saving (ruining) surgeries.

4. *Do you have your own in-house engine or use a third party system? If third party, which one do you use?*

   Both. We use various external technologies as they make sense, though lately we've mostly used Unity. Our internal technology focuses on the server side support of multiplayer gaming, which is a key area for us. We call this package of solutions allowing seamless cross-platform play Bossa Frictionless Gaming . . . just because that is abbreviated to BFG.

5. *Which platforms do you release on now / plan to release on?*

   Our primary focus is to create games for PC (Linux, Win and Mac) and touch devices. We're particularly interested in multi-platform games, where players can easily access the same game universe from various devices. Consoles are always an interesting consideration, but due to the locked nature of these platforms, Bossa hasn't released a game there yet.

6. *Which is your most successful platform so far?*

   Based on the titles we've done to date, PC is the strongest, but our tablet and phone games are also doing very well.

7. *What are the development tools you use most (i.e. 2D, 3D software, audio tools etc.)?*

   We like to pick and choose the tools to match what we want to achieve rather than designing games around pre-existing limitations. Having said that, the core development tools we use are what you'd expect: artists use Maya, zBrush, Photoshop and Illustrator amongst other tools, whilst programmers rely on a range of Unity extensions and a bunch of software development applications like Git, Jenkins and others.

8. *What advice would you give to a new studio?*

   Remain focused but be ready to change direction!

   I know this sounds contradictory but really, they're just two sides of the same coin. Our experience here at Bossa was that you have to have a strong vision to succeed. Without that focus, you often find yourself running around in circles and wasting time doing things that don't help you in making a better game.

This doesn't mean that you shouldn't change! Constant experimentation with various solutions to achieve your goals is essential, and you even want to review your higher-level goals on a regular basis. But you need to make sure that you ask the right questions and make changes for the right reasons.

Gaming changes with a lightning speed—if you're slowing yourself with unnecessary sidetracks or forgot to keep in touch with the environment your game is arriving to, you are doomed to fail.

9. *What marketing resources do you use?*

Building and maintaining a close relationship with our community of players was a very important focus for Bossa from day one. That's why one of the founders is an expert in PR, marketing and communication. Our efforts to engage with our players is a useful way to measure what our audience wants, but it's also a very rewarding exercise for the team. We're active in various social media channels, and we try to attend as many gaming events as we possibly can. Nothing can replace these firsthand experiences, and it's a great way to say thanks to our players who make our games successful. Surgeon Simulator is the perfect example, we made a funny game but it was our players who made it into a success by creating nearly a million individual videos on YouTube.

10. *What are your favourite indie games sites?*

The editorial process of sites can make it easier to digest large amounts of information fast. But I prefer to follow my favourite indie developers and promising games directly on Twitter and their sites. Never before was it this easy to get insight directly from creators of your favourite games, and I don't want to miss out.

11. *Any mistakes/hiccups you have made so far, something you would advise a new studio to avoid?*

As I said before, the right balance between focus and flexibility is important. And we definitely learnt a lot of lessons there. Even though we have founded Bossa on those principles, looking back now with hindsight, I can see how we failed them here and there by sticking to ideas we should have let go of or went around in circles instead of making a strong decision fast. Ultimately though, it's a learning process. The trick is to avoid making the same mistakes over and over again.

Game Legal Text

It is a good idea to include certain legal texts within every game you develop. This helps to confirm the copyright of the product, and happily doesn't really take any time or effort to implement.

You should display the copyright notices in the following places:

1. Title screen
2. End of game credits
   ©[Current Year] [Company Name]. ALL RIGHTS RESERVED.

Additionally, it is a good idea to include a legal screen after boot. The purpose of this is to display more detailed text that would otherwise clutter the layout of busier screens like the title screen.

Below is an example of a more detailed legal text, which also covers the game name, logo and third party copyrights:

©[Current Year] [Company Name], [Game Name], its logo and all related logos and slogans are copyright [Company Name]. All other logos are copyright of their respective owners. ALL RIGHTS RESERVED.

Registered Trademarks

If your game name is a registered trademark, replace the © symbol with the relevant ® mark.

Business Consultancy and Agency Representation

In principal, an agent is there to represent a developer and help place their product with a good publisher or distribution service and get the best deal possible. The good ones should help you build up your business, and avoid many of the common pitfalls when negotiating publishing and distribution agreements.

Arise, Games Consultancy Services!

In recent years, agencies have had to adapt to the many changes in the development model and the increase in self-publishing. As such, they now tend to offer a broader range of services including consultancy, business advice and production services.

If you can get a good agent, they can be a great asset as they will most likely negotiate a better deal than you would yourself. As such, agencies can be very selective with whom they work, so you'll need to impress them with your games and team.

Below I have listed the agents that have been recommended by both developers and publishers. These are generally regarded as the best in the business, and as such they should be your first ports of call.

DDM—Jeff Hilbert
Website: http://www.ddmagents.com
Contact: jeff.hilbert@ddmagents.com
Jeff knows just about everyone and is very well respected. Very efficient and gets the job done but only represents top tier developers (or those aiming to be top tier).

Interactive Studio Management (ISM)
Website: http://www.ism-agency.com
Contact: Online form
ISM is more of a traditional agency dealing with larger AAA titles.

Flashman Studios
Website: http://www.flashmanstudios.com
Contact: sales@flashmanstudios.com or tony@flashmanstudios.com
Tony is a nice guy with a good reputation; I understand they look after their studios well.

Dan Adelman
Website: http://dan-adelman.com
Contact: dan@dan-adelman.com

Dan used to be the head of Nintendo of America's digital distribution business, helping facilitate the launch of hundreds of games. Dan offers a variety of consultancy services for all phases for development.

The Arsenal Agency
Website: http://www.thearsenalagency.com
Contact: info@thearsenalagency.com
These guys only came to my attention at the time or writing, but Caspar Grey, the associate there, has been in publisher bizdev for years.

Tenshi Consulting
Website: http://www.tenshiconsulting.com
Contact: partners@tenshipartners.com

Tenshi are more of a business consultancy, offering a wide range of services to help develop your studio. These include mentoring and investment readiness programmes for start-ups, support in accessing finance and grant funding and supporting the delivery of specific projects.

And that's a wrap! Thanks for reading, and I wish you every success in the future. Take care fellow indie developer!

Index

Printed and bound by CPI Group (UK) Ltd, Croydon, CR0 4YY

22/10/2024

01777624-0003